S a v o r i n g  *t h e W i l d*

Game, Fish, and Wild Plant Cookery

FALCON®

HELENA, MONTANA

Contents

© 1989 by Falcon® Publishing Co., Inc., Helena & Billings, Montana.

All rights reserved, including the right to reproduce any part of this book in any form, except brief quotations for reviews, without written permission of the publisher.

Editing, design, and other prepress work by Falcon®, Helena, Montana.
Printed in Canada.

Library of Congress Catalog Card Number: 95-61747
ISBN: 1-56044-573-4

For additional copies of this book, please visit your local bookstore or write Falcon, P.O. Box 1718, Helena, MT 59624. You may also call toll-free 1-800-582-2665.
To contact us via e-mail, visit our website at http:\\www.falconguide.com

edible wild plants

MUCH MORE THAN MUSHROOMS

2 cups sliced fresh mushrooms, preferably meadow
mushrooms—Chanterelles or Boletus might be
substituted
4 tablespoons butter
$^1/_2$ cup chopped onion
$^1/_2$ cup chopped celery
$^1/_2$ cup chopped green pepper
$^3/_4$ teaspoon salt
dash pepper
2 tablespoons minced fresh parsley
$^1/_2$ cup mayonnaise
6 slices stale bread, preferably whole wheat
3 eggs
$1^1/_2$ cups whole milk
1 cup grated sharp cheddar cheese
$^1/_2$ teaspoon dry mustard

Sauté mushrooms in butter 5 minutes. Add vegetables, cook another 5 minutes. Remove from heat and add mayonnaise. Oil inside of 2-quart casserole. Beginning with a bread layer, alternate layers of the vegetable mixture and grated cheese, saving some of the cheese for topping.

Beat eggs lightly; add milk, mustard, salt, and pepper. Pour over the casserole and sprinkle remaining cheese on top. Bake, uncovered, in 350° oven about 45 minutes, or until custard is set and top lightly browned. Cool 5 minutes before serving.
—Fran Davis, Otis Orchards, WA

PICKLED MUSHROOMS

2 pounds (approximately)
any good, solid fresh
mushroom
$^3/_4$ cup vinegar
$1^1/_2$ cups water
$^1/_3$ cup sugar

$1^1/_2$ teaspoons salt
$^1/_2$ teaspoon ginger
1 teaspoon whole cloves
1 teaspoon whole allspice
garlic salt

Mix vinegar, water, sugar, salt and ginger and bring to boil. Clean mushrooms and place in large bowl. (Larger mushrooms may be cut into cubes.) Pour hot syrup over mushrooms and set aside until mushrooms shrink. Pack in small jars, adding one or two cloves, pinch of allspice and dash of garlic salt to each jar. Seal tightly with lids. Cure at least one week before using.
—Fran Davis, Otis Orchards, WA

MUSHROOMS IN VERMOUTH

3/4 cup dry vermouth
1/3 cup salad oil
4 tablespoons lemon juice
1 teaspoon salt
1/4 teaspoon pepper
1 tablespoon grated onion

1 tablespoon chopped parsley
1 pound fresh button mushrooms—meadow mushrooms, wild or commercial

Clean mushrooms; cut off stem tips. Combine other ingredients in a large bowl. Add mushrooms to marinade; cover and refrigerate 24–36 hours. Stir or shake bowl occasionally. To serve, drain and place in serving bowl. Provide toothpicks.
—Fran Davis, Otis Orchards, WA

SHAGGY MANES BAKED IN CREAM

Clean the shaggy manes. Slice in half, lengthwise. Layer in shallow baking dish. Pour 1 cup of heavy cream or 1 small can of evaporated milk over the top. Top with crumbled Ritz crackers and a small amount of grated cheese. Sprinkle with salt and pepper. Bake in 300° oven, uncovered, for about 20 minutes.
—Fran Davis, Otis Orchards, WA

DEEP FRIED CORAL HYNDUM

Separate fungi into small clusters. Prepare a thin batter from pancake flour, according to package instructions. Dip fungi into batter, drop into hot oil, and fry until brown.
—Fran Davis, Otis Orchards, WA

SAUTÉED MUSHROOMS

1 pound mushrooms
2 tablespoons butter
1 tablespoon oil
salt
pepper

Remove the stems from the mushrooms. Heat the butter and oil over moderately high heat until it is bubbly and starts to spatter. Don't allow it to brown.

Place the stems in the skillet and sauté for 5 minutes. Add the mushroom caps, round side down. Don't add more oil, although the mushrooms, will absorb most of it immediately. Shake pan.

After 2 minutes, turn caps over and shake skillet from time to time. Sauté for 3 more minutes. Sprinkle with salt and pepper before serving. Don't cover if the mushrooms must wait for other food. (A cover will cause a change in texture and the mushrooms will release their juices.) If they must be rewarmed, heat for 1 minute only.

More oil is needed if mushroom slices are to be sautéed. If the mushrooms are small, the stems may be left on the caps, but the pound should be cooked in 2 groups, using half the butter and oil each time.—*Montana Outdoors*

JEAN'S MUSHROOMS ORIENTAL

⅓ pound mushrooms, sliced
½ stick butter (2 ounces)
1 package frozen green peas
½ cup sliced onion
1 can bean sprouts
1 small can water chestnuts, sliced in half

1 can cream of mushroom soup
1 teaspoon salt
½ teaspoon pepper
⅔ cup milk
1 small can of Chinese noodles

Sauté mushrooms in the butter. Combine all other ingredients, except the Chinese noodles, and mix with the mushroom mixture. Pour into a casserole and bake at 350° for 40 minutes. Top with Chinese noodles and serve. (When doubling the recipe, use three packages of frozen peas, while just doubling the other ingredients.)—Jean Applegate, Helena, MT

MUSHROOM SPAGHETTI SAUCE

½ pound mushrooms
1 clove garlic
1 10-ounce can tomato
  puree
1 6-ounce can tomato
  paste
2 tablespoons olive oil

½ teaspoon oregano
½ teaspoon sweet basil
½ teaspoon salt
⅛ teaspoon pepper
½ teaspoon sugar
¼ cup water

Slice the mushrooms. Mince the clove of garlic, then mash. Place all ingredients in a saucepan and mix. Bring to a quick boil and lower the heat. Gently simmer the sauce, 5–7 minutes.
—*Montana Outdoors*

POLISH SAUERKRAUT

2 cups canned sauerkraut
½ pound bulk sausage
1 cup chopped mushrooms—meadow mushrooms,
  Chanterelles or Boletus are best
1 large onion, chopped

Boil sauerkraut until tender. Crumble sausage and brown thoroughly. In separate skillet, brown chopped mushrooms and onion. Drain sausage and sauerkraut. Combine all ingredients. Serves 4.—Fran Davis, Otis Orchards, WA

CREAM OF WATERCRESS SOUP

1 pound potatoes, peeled and diced
1 pound leeks, cleaned thoroughly and sliced,
    including the tender green portions
5 cups chicken broth
salt
1½ cup firmly packed, cleaned, and chopped watercress
½–1 cup cream
chives or parsley

Place the potatoes, leeks, and chicken broth in a large kettle; bring to a boil. Gently simmer for 1 hour or until vegetables are very tender. Add the watercress and cook for about 5 minutes more. Add salt; oversalt slightly since this is a chilled soup. In small batches, put the soup in a blender; blend until smooth.

After blending, place the soup in a large bowl. Add cream until soup is desired consistency. Chill thoroughly. Before serving, garnish with freshly snipped chives or chopped parsley.
—Kay Ellerhoff, Helena, MT

CAMAS BULB—THREE WAYS

Camas bulb is starchy and nutritious and probably best in the fall. However, it is usually dug in the spring, when its blue flowers are visible so that it is not confused with the death camas—which has white flowers and otherwise closely resemble "blue" camas.

Baked camas bulb—Wrap in foil and bake in 325° oven 10–20 minutes, depending on the size of the bulb, usually 1–2 inches in diameter. Bake until tender. Serve as you would a baked potato with butter and salt. This method can also be used when camping by utilizing the coals from the campfire.

Boiled camas bulb—Boil in a small amount of water, 10–15 minutes or until tender.

Raw camas bulb—Cut greens and roots off, wash thoroughly, and eat as is.—Mary Conklin, Helena, MT

SHEPHERD'S PURSE

The young leaves should be boiled for about 20 minutes, with at least 1 change of water. Older leaves tend to have a strong taste, so gather only the young shoots and leaves. Eat like spinach, with a little salt and vinegar.

Since this plant (*Capsella bursa-pastoris*) grows in waste areas, collect where insecticides and herbicides have not been used.
—Jim Bayne, Bozeman, MT

CANDIED WILD GINGER ROOT

Gather the runners that lie on the surface of the ground, just under the mat of leaves. Clean off any leaves and wash thoroughly. Cut into 1-inch lengths. Barely cover with water and simmer until tender, about 1 hour. For each cup of root, add 1 cup white sugar. Boil about 30 minutes, or until the syrup is consumed. Spread candied root out on a cookie sheet and allow to dry for a day or so. It should become crusty and dry. Store in airtight jars. Eaten as a snack, it aids digestion.—Fran Davis, Otis Orchards, WA

DEEP FRIED DANDELION BLOSSOMS

Gather full flowers, away from roads, fields, or lawns that have been sprayed with any type of chemical fertilizer or weed killer. Prepare pancake batter (a small amount) according to manufacturer's instructions. Dip blossoms into batter one at a time, and drop into hot oil. Fry until golden brown. Serve hot.

Clusters of elderberry blossoms may be prepared in this same manner. Wash the clusters, shake dry, dip into the pancake batter, and fry.—Fran Davis, Otis Orchards, WA

OYSTER PLANT

Clean the white tap roots thoroughly and boil in a small amount of water until tender, 30–60 minutes. The roots, even when done, are a little chewy. Add whole milk, 4 cups milk to 1 cup of roots, and heat, but don't boil. Add butter, salt and pepper to taste.

The final product will resemble oyster stew. If the plants are too old, the stew will taste bitter.—Jim Bayne, Bozeman, MT

WILD FRUIT DUMPLINGS

Wild elderberries, blueberries or serviceberries are all good in this dessert. (Other berries—such as blackberries or strawberries may also be used.) Stew the fruit until cooked, adding enough sugar to sweeten to taste. Mix the following batter:

½ cup flour
2 teaspoons baking powder
dash salt
1 tablespoon sugar
1 egg
¼ cup milk

Mix well. It should be fairly thick. Drop by teaspoonsful into boiling fruit; cover tightly and simmer 15 minutes. Serve with a hard sauce made by creaming together 1 cup brown sugar and ¼ cup butter or margarine. This recipe makes about 4 medium dumplings; it may be doubled. Best served when hot.
—Fran Davis, Otis Orchards, WA

ROSEHIP JELLY

1 pint rosehips, cleaned
peelings from 2 tart apples

Cover the rosehips and peelings with water and cook until tender. Crush and let drip through a jelly bag.

2 cups rosehip juice
2 cups sugar
½ cup lemon juice
paraffin

Measure out 2 cups juice; add the sugar and bring to the boiling point. Add the lemon juice and boil briskly 12–15 minutes. Test after 10 minutes, as the liquid toughens if boiled too long.

Rosehips should be gathered in late summer or early fall after the flowers have lost their petals.
—Mrs. Clarence Kinney, Missoula, MT

ROSEHIP SYRUP

Combine 1 quart rosehips and 2 cups water. Boil for 15 minutes. Strain through double thickness of cheesecloth. (Add some pulp to the juice for additional flavor.) Combine 2 cups juice with 2 cups sugar. Boil for 1 minute.—Cathy Ellis, Tucson, Ariz.

ROSEHIP TEA

Grind approximately 3–4 cups of rosehips. Boil in 2–3 cups of water for 20 minutes. Strain the liquid to remove the pulp. It's delicious either hot or cold.—Jim Bayne, Bozeman, MT

ROSE PETAL JAM

If you want roses in winter, make some rose petal jam and store it away for a cold, wintry day.

Gather rose petals from any fragrant variety; red is the best color. Cut away the white portion at the base of each petal because it is bitter. Place 1 cup petals, well packed, into a blender. Add $^3/_4$ cup water and the juice of 1 lemon. Blend until smooth. Gradually add $2^1/_2$ cups sugar. Let the blender run until all the sugar is dissolved.

Stir 1 package of SureJell commercial pectin into $^3/_4$ cup water and boil for 1 minute. Add to the rose-sugar mixture and blend slowly until the ingredients are thoroughly mixed. Pour into small jars. Let stand at room temperature for about 6 hours or until jelled. Keep refrigerated or it may be frozen and kept indefinitely.
—Fran Davis, Otis Orchards, WA

CHOKECHERRY JELLY

Cover clean chokecherries with water; simmer until tender. Crush the berries and allow the mixture to drip through a jelly bag, or through several layers of cheesecloth. Measure juice.

Follow directions on pectin package for preparation of sour cherry jelly.—Mary Conklin, Helena, MT

CHOKECHERRY SYRUP

Measure equal amounts of juice and sugar; bring to a boil. Pour into hot jars and seal.—Mary Conklin, Helena, MT

CHOKECHERRY WINE

Pour 2 gallons of water over 1 gallon of chokecherries. Let ferment for 12 days.

Strain and add 1 gallon of sugar to each 2 gallons of juice. Put in a warm place and let the sugar work out. It requires 2 weeks or more. Bottle and store.

This recipe makes a sweet wine. Experiment to obtain the sweetness you like.—Glen Bayne, Livingston, MT

FLOWERING HAWTHORN APPLE JELLY

Wash the fruit thoroughly. Barely cover with water; boil until the fruit gives off its juice. Drain through a jelly bag. (You will need 5 cups juice.)

5 cups juice
7 cups sugar
the juice of 1 lemon
5 drops oil of cloves
1 bottle Certo

Combine the juice and sugar. Bring to a full rolling boil. Add the lemon juice and oil of cloves. Add the Certo and boil 1 minute. Pour into jelly glasses and seal. This makes a delightful pale pink jelly that is delicious with meat.

The flowering hawthorn produces a bright red-rose fruit about the size of a pie cherry. Do not gather overly ripe fruit, as it will not jell properly.—Fran Davis, Otis Orchards, WA

BUFFALOBERRY JELLY

Wash and crush berries and add $^1/_2$ cup water per 2 quarts of fruit. Boil slowly 10 minutes, stirring occasionally. Pour into jelly bag and drain off juice. To each cup of juice add 1 cup sugar. Bring to a boil and boil until it jells. (Test with a spoon; when 2 drips form on the spoon, this jelly is ready.)

Gather berries in the fall after a frost; otherwise they are very bitter.—Jim Bayne, Bozeman, MT

PYRACANTHA BERRY JELLY

Wash the orange-red berries thoroughly. Barely cover with water; boil until the juice is a rich orange color. Drain through a jelly bag. (You will need 2 cups juice.)

    2 cups juice
    3 cups sugar
    ¼ cup (scant) lemon juice
    2 tablespoons vinegar
    ½ bottle Certo

Bring the juice, sugar, lemon juice and vinegar to a full rolling boil. Add the Certo and boil hard for 2 minutes. Pour into jelly glasses or baby food jars and seal. Makes a beautiful pale orange jelly.

The pyracantha is commercially grown yard tree, producing large umbels of bright orange-red fruit in late fall. It lasts all winter and is consumed by winter foraging birds.
—Fran Davis, Otis Orchards, WA

RORTE BAER

    1 pound huckleberries (4 cups)
    2 cups sugar

Mix together the huckleberries and sugar, using an electric mixer, until the juices run and the berries are reduced to a pulp. The berries absorb the sugar, which acts like a preservative.

If you don't have an electric mixer, combine the berries and sugar and stir whenever you happen to walk by. Continue for three days. Pack in sterilized jars.—*Montana Outdoors*

s   m   a   l   l   g   a   m   e

SQUIRREL CREOLE

1 squirrel
1 medium onion, sliced
1 garlic clove, chopped
1 tablespoon shortening
1 large can tomatoes with juice
$1/2$ teaspoon salt
$1/2$ cup milk
1 cup flour, sifted
1 teaspoon salt
$1/4$ teaspoon pepper
4–6 tablespoons shortening
green pepper rings
corn relish

Sauté onion, garlic in melted shortening in heavy skillet until onion is golden brown. Strain tomato pulp from juice. Add tomato pulp and salt to browned onion and garlic. Simmer very gently. Cut squirrel into serving pieces. Dip into milk, then roll in flour seasoned with salt and pepper. Brown floured pieces in melted shortening. When browned, cover squirrel with tomato sauce; slowly add strained tomato juice, and simmer gently until squirrel is tender, $1-1^1/2$ hours. Garnish with green pepper rings filled with corn relish.—National Rifle Association *Centennial Cookbook*

CURRIED RACCOON

2 young raccoons
3 tablespoons butter
4 tablespoons curry
  powder
2 cups chicken stock
2 large tomatoes, diced
3 medium onions, chopped
1 tablespoon paprika

1 bay leaf
$1/4$ teaspoon Tabasco
  sauce
1 inch of stick cinnamon
1 tablespoon salt
1 lemon, sliced thinly
1 cup sour cream

Parboil raccoon in salted water to which has been added 1 medium onion, quartered, and ¹/₄ teaspoon Tabasco sauce. Cool raccoon; remove meat from bones and cut in 1-inch cubes. Brown butter in skillet; add curry powder, meat; stir over heat until dark. Add stock, tomatoes, onions, seasonings and lemon; mix well and simmer until meat is tender. Reduce heat and add sour cream. Heat thoroughly but do not boil.
—National Rifle Association *Centennial Cookbook*

BARBECUED BEAVER

1 beaver, cut in serving pieces
3 tablespoons salt
3 tablespoons butter, melted
1 medium onion, chopped
1 teaspoon salt
¹/₂ teaspoon garlic salt
¹/₄ teaspoon paprika
¹/₄ teaspoon hot pepper sauce
¹/₄ teaspoon dry mustard
¹/₄ cup catsup
3 tablespoons Worcestershire sauce
3 tablespoons cider vinegar
1 tablespoon celery flakes
¹/₈ teaspoon thyme
¹/₄ teaspoon marjoram

Remove all fat from beaver and cut in serving pieces. Soak 3–4 hours in water to which has been added 2 rounded tablespoons of salt. Place beaver in large kettle; cover with water, add 1 tablespoon salt. Slowly simmer 1 hour. Remove from kettle and rinse meat. Place in roaster. Mix next 10 ingredients, pour over meat. Scatter celery flakes, thyme and marjoram over top. Bake, covered, in 200° oven 3 hours. Turn every half hour.
—National Rifle Association *Centennial Cookbook*

WOODCHUCK MULLIGAN

4 pounds woodchuck
5 cups cold water
1 tablespoon salt
3/4 cup rice
1 1/2 cups diced celery
1 cup diced carrots
1/2 teaspoon pepper
1/4 teaspoon paprika

Place the meat in a gallon kettle, adding the water and half of the salt. Cover. Simmer for 3 hours or more until the meat is tender. Remove meat and strain the broth. Cut the meat in cubes. Heat the broth to boiling. Add the remaining salt, rice, pepper, celery and carrots. Cover and cook rapidly for 10–15 minutes until rice and vegetables are tender. Add meat, heat thoroughly, and sprinkle with paprika. Serve at once.
—National Rifle Association *Centennial Cookbook*

MUSKRAT SWEET & SOUR

1 muskrat, skinned
   and cleaned
1 large onion, chopped
1 teaspoon dry mustard
1 teaspoon allspice
1 teaspoon salt
1/2 teaspoon pepper

3/4 cup catsup
4 beef bouillon cubes
4 cups water
5 gingersnaps
3/4 cup vinegar
3/4 cup brown sugar

Cut prepared muskrat in serving pieces. Parboil and scrape off all fat. Place the pieces in a roasting pan adding onion. Sprinkle with mustard, allspice, salt, and pepper. In separate pan, heat catsup, bouillon cubes, water, gingersnaps, vinegar, and brown sugar. Pour over muskrat pieces and roast covered in 350° oven until done, about 2 hours. Serves 6.
—National Rifle Association *Centennial Cookbook*

ROASTED RABBIT—CAJUN STYLE

1 rabbit, whole
salt, pepper, combined herbs and spices
vinegar
1 onion, cut in half
3 tablespoons oil
optional—sweet potatoes; small, whole onions;
    2 cans green peas

Clean thoroughly; salt and pepper rather heavily—do not cut the rabbit in parts. Disjoint by breaking rabbit in half. If the game taste is desired, allow to stand overnight, or at least one hour before cooking with salt and pepper on. If a gamey taste is not desired, cover with water and sprinkle vinegar into water rather heavily. Before cooking, pour liquid off. An onion, cut in half, or combined herbs and spices can be added to the soaking solution. If so, the rabbit is rinsed off and resalted lightly.

Place halved rabbit in pot and cover with water. Allow to boil until all the water has boiled away. Add more water if necessary to cook the rabbit until fork-tender. When the rabbit is tender, allow any remaining water to completely boil away and begin to sizzle. Add the oil and lower heat. Stir continuously as it browns. If it begins to stick to pot, add a dash of water. You may want to add some quartered sweet potatoes or small, whole onions, cooking until tender. Remove the onions, chop, and cook with green peas, as an added accompaniment.

—Elise Wildey, Lafitte, LA (from *Idaho Wildlife Review*)

RABBIT STEW A LA CAJUN

1 rabbit, cut in parts
1 large onion, chopped
1–3 cloves of garlic
1 can whole tomatoes
piece of sweet pepper
3 tablespoons oil
2 tablespoons flour
optional—carrots, Irish potatoes, celery;
   2–3 tablespoons parsley, chopped

Place the oil in a large pot. When it is hot, lower the temperature and stir in 2 heaping tablespoons of flour. Continue stirring until the roux is the color of rich milk chocolate. Remove from heat; add the rabbit, onion, and garlic, and return pot to burner. Continue stirring until it begins to stick. Then add a dash of water, tomatoes, and sweet pepper. Turn up heat until contents begin to boil. Add 2 quarts of water and lower to medium heat and simmer.

As the rabbit becomes fork-tender, the total amount of stew liquid should be just enough to cover the rabbit. Any more will make the stew too watery, so keep the liquid at this level. Now add carrots, Irish potatoes, celery if you wish—or use only 1 vegetable of your choice. When the vegetables are tender, sprinkle with the parsley.
—Elise Wildey, Lafitte, LA. (from *Idaho Wildlife Review*)

CABBAGE AND RABBIT CASSEROLE

1 rabbit, whole
3 generous tablespoons oil
1 large onion, chopped
1 large cabbage, sectioned or quartered
salt, to taste
1 can whole tomatoes
cooked rice

Prepare the rabbit by salting it heavily. Roast it in the oil; when it is nice and brown, add the onion. Place a portion of the cabbage in the pot on top of the rabbit; cover pot until cabbage wilts. Then stir well, add more cabbage, wait until it wilts, etc. until all cabbage is in the pot. (When first adding the cabbage check to see if it is sticking; you may need to add a slight amount of water, although the cabbage provides some water in the process of cooking.) When the cabbage begins to brown, you may need to add another tablespoon of oil to brown it well.

Add salt to taste and the tomatoes; cook for $^1/_2$ hour more. Serve over hot rice.
—Elise Wildey, Lafitte, LA. (from *Idaho Wildlife Review*)

RABBIT PIE

    1 rabbit, washed and cut into 4 pieces
    salt, to taste
    1 small onion, minced
    3 tablespoons butter
    4 tablespoons flour
    2 cups cooking liquid
    1 pie crust (top)

Barely cover the rabbit with water. With a lid on, simmer until tender, adding salt to taste. Drain the liquid and save for later.

Bone the rabbit, leaving the meat in fairly large chunks. Sauté the onion in the butter. Add the flour, stirring until smooth. Gradually add the cooking liquid. Bring slowly to a boil, cooking 2 minutes more. Add the pieces of rabbit, pour into a baking dish and cover with your favorite pie crust recipe or a mix. Bake at 350° for 35 minutes.—from *The 1974 Rod and Gun Calendar*, submitted by R. H. Turnbull, Helena, MT

HASENPFEFFER

2 rabbits, cut in serving
   pieces
1 cup vinegar, mixed
   with ¹/₂ cup water
1¹/₂ cups red wine
2 cups sliced onion
salt and pepper, to taste
1 tablespoon powdered
   mustard

1 tablespoon pickling spice
4 slices bacon
flour
¹/₂ stick butter
   or margarine
1 tablespoon sugar
1 cup (or more) sour
   cream

Marinate rabbit in vinegar, water, wine, onion, pepper, salt, mustard, and pickling spice 2 days in refrigerator, turning now and then. Remove from marinade, dry, flour, and brown lightly in butter. Place rabbit back in casserole with marinade. Wrap bacon around pieces. Bake in 300° oven 2¹/₂ hours, or until tender. Remove meat onto platter and keep warm. Add sugar to marinade, cook down, and make a mixture of butter and flour to thicken. Add sour cream. Heat, but do not boil. Pour over rabbit and serve with noodles or dumplings. Serves 6.
—Nancy Krenz, *New Mexico Wildlife*

FRIED RABBIT

dressed rabbit, cut into pieces
1 cup flour
1 teaspoon salt
¹/₄ teaspoon pepper
2 tablespoons salad oil
1 tablespoon butter
1 chicken bouillon cube
¹/₂ cup hot water

Dredge rabbit pieces in seasoned flour until well-coated. Brown on all sides in the salad oil and butter in skillet. Dissolve bouillon cube in the hot water and pour over the meat. Cover and cook for 45 minutes over low heat.—Mrs. L. Ramsdell, Lemmon, SD (from *Cooking the Sportsman's Harvest*)

g a m e   b i r d s

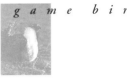

GAME BIRDS—FIELD DRESSING
TO FREEZER

If you're an avid bird hunter like I am, you have tramped through your share of fields, briars, and sloughs, and cleaned your share of wildfowl. Chances are also pretty good that you have seen a few game birds ruined before they reached the table.

Two classic examples of mishandling are the hunter who stacks his limit of birds together in the closed trunk of a car on a hot day or carries several birds in a hot, rubber-lined game pocket, leaving the birds to "cook" and perhaps spoil by the day's end. Such practices guarantee noticeable changes in the quality of your table fare —all bad.

Fortunately, a modest dash of common sense is all that's required to properly care for any game bird. First, cool the body heat from the birds as quickly as possible and keep that temperature down until the birds are cleaned. Field dressing is relatively simple and doesn't take long. Pull out the feathers from below the breast bone to the anal opening. Then make a cut through the skin and muscle starting below the breast bone, continuing down to the anal opening. Reach in and remove the internal organs, pulling down toward the anal opening. Be sure to take out the windpipe and crop.

Some hunters prefer to pack the empty cavity with dry grass to absorb blood and prevent flies from crawling into the body cavity during warm weather.

Next, we examine the controversial question of whether to hang the birds in a shady nook for a couple of days or so to properly age. I tend to agree with an old hunting buddy of mine who maintains that, "Hanging should be reserved for horse thieves." In the past, hanging birds to age and tenderize them was a traditional "must". The practice stemmed from lack of refrigeration and liberal limits. I'm sure I would have advocated the use of the aging process during that era if I had faced plucking and cleaning a score or more of grouse and ducks after a day's hunt. Most of the game birds shot by scatter gunners are juveniles or birds of the year and not tough old birds, as many believe. The aging process might have some merit for slightly tenderizing some of the "old-timers" we occasionally bring home, but I've been unable to detect any difference.

A second area of controversy centers around whether to skin or pluck a game bird.

I prefer to dry pluck my birds. Granted, it's faster to skin a game bird than it is to pluck it, but did you ever buy a skinned chicken? When you remove the skin, the fat and much of the flavor go with it. However some birds such as a mature sage grouse "bomber" or some types of waterfowl are more palatable when skinned.

Pluck the game as soon as possible after field dressing. The feathers will come out faster with less chance of tearing the skin. Hold the bird's back firmly with one hand and start picking feathers in the chest region. Pull the feathers toward the head with fast, deliberate jerks to avoid tearing the skin. When you finish the underside of the bird, start on the back and proceed to the legs and neck. The hardest part of the plucking operation is removing wing feathers. If the game bird is in the "small" category, simply cut the wing off flush with the bird's body, using a pair of pruning shears. Also use the shears to cut off the legs and wings at the joints. Finally, remove the head and terminal end of the bird's body.

Singe off remaining pinfeathers over a camp stove or with "farmer" matches. Don't make the mistake of singeing them over your gas burners inside the house—the odor of burnt feathers lingers for a long time.

Rinse the birds in cold water to remove blood clots and fragmentary organs such as lungs and kidneys not properly removed in the field dressing operation. Wipe the birds inside and out with a paper towel before freezing.

Although transparent plastic bags are probably the easiest way to package a game bird for freezing, I prefer to freeze my birds in water to prevent freezer burn. A pheasant or mallard just fits a half gallon milk carton. Put the birds in first, cover with cold water and quick freeze them. Label the package with a marking pencil to identify the kind of bird and the packaging date.

It pays to treat your game birds properly in this day and age. They're well worth it! Not only will they taste better, but if you want to look at the cold economics, just add up the costs of your bird hunting trips for the past season. The price of each bird which ends up on your dining table might be a real persuader to taking better care of your game birds.—Ken Walcheck

SWEET AND SOUR GROUSE

1 sage grouse or 2 sharptails
1 tablespoon instant minced onion
1 cup catsup
1 cup water
1 teaspoon salt
1 teaspoon paprika
2 tablespoons Worcestershire sauce
4 tablespoons vinegar
4 tablespoons brown sugar
2 teaspoons dry mustard

Combine all ingredients, except grouse, and heat. Prepare cooking bag according to manufacturer's instructions. Place whole grouse in bag and pour in sauce. Puncture bag. Bake in 350° oven 1$^{1}/_{2}$ hours. Split cooking bag. Baste and cook another $^{1}/_{2}$ hour.

For a low calorie sauce, substitute Sugar Twin Brown Sugar for the regular brown sugar.—Dick Trueblood, Glasgow, MT

SMOTHERED GROUSE

2 grouse
flour, seasoned with salt and pepper
½ cup fat
1 cup milk or light cream
2 teaspoons onion flakes
2 teaspoons diced carrots
sour cream

Cut the grouse into serving pieces. Roll in the flour. Brown pieces slowly in a large skillet in the hot fat.

Pour the milk or light cream into the skillet. Cover and cook over low heat about 1 hour, or until tender. Place in a casserole with the onion flakes and carrots. Add enough sour cream to cover. Cook for another hour in medium oven, 325–350°.
—*The Great Outdoors*

CINNAMON–HONEY GRILLED GROUSE

2 grouse, quartered and previously soaked in salt water
    (4 tablespoons salt and enough water to cover grouse.
    They should be soaked at least 4 hours before cooking.)
⅓ cup water
1 cup dry sherry
¾ cup honey
4 teaspoons cinnamon
2 teaspoons curry powder
2 teaspoons garlic salt

Rinse grouse and place in shallow baking pan. Combine ingredients for marinade and blend well; pour over grouse. Cover and allow to stand at room temperature 2–3 hours. Bake in 300 degree oven 2 hours. Remove from oven; place grouse on grill over hot coals. Baste often with reserved marinade, turning at least every 20 minutes. Serves 4–5.—Nancy Krenz, *New Mexico Wildlife*

WILD DUCK A LA NEW MEXICO

2 ducks, cleaned and soaked in salt water (4 tablespoons
   salt and enough water to cover ducks. They should be
   soaked at least 4 hours before cooking.)

<u>Stuffing</u>
4$^1/_2$ cups soft bread crumbs
1 cup finely chopped celery
1 cup finely chopped onion
1 cup chopped pecans
salt, to taste
$^1/_2$ teaspoon poultry seasoning
$^1/_2$ cup milk, scalded

<u>Chili Sauce Mixture</u>
1 cup catsup
$^1/_2$ cup Worcestershire sauce
$^1/_4$ cup A-1 sauce
$^1/_2$ cup pureed mild red chili

Rinse ducks, stuff, and wrap in bacon. Cover with aluminum foil.
Roast at 300° for 3$^1/_2$ hours. Baste with chili sauce mixture during
last half hour. When serving, have remaining chili sauce hot in
small dish to spoon over. Serves 4.
—Nancy Krenz, *New Mexico Wildlife*

ROAST WILD DUCK WITH STUFFING

2 wild ducks, cleaned
1 cup chopped onion
1 cup chopped celery
$^3/_4$ stick butter or margarine
4 cups dry bread cubes
1$^1/_2$ teaspoons salt
$^1/_2$ teaspoon pepper
1 teaspoon sage
8 pieces of bacon

Melt butter or margarine in heavy skillet over low heat; add onion and celery and sauté slowly until onion is transparent. Put bread cubes in a large bowl; add salt, pepper, and sage. Add enough water to the onion-celery mixture to make dressing quite moist. Bring to a quick boil and pour over bread cubes; toss. Makes enough stuffing for 2 ducks.

Season ducks generously with salt and pepper, inside and out. Add dressing and close the cavity. Place ducks, breast down, in a large roasting pan, uncovered. Place 4 pieces of bacon across each duck. Roast at 325° for 3–3$^1/_2$ hours or until skin is crisp and dark brown.—Esther and Don Brown, Bozeman, MT.

WILD DUCK

    1 wild duck
    cooked wild rice
    raw apple, diced
    prunes
    orange chunks
    butter
    Burgundy

Skin the duck. Stuff with a mixture of the wild rice, apple, prunes and orange chunks. Cover and roast in a very hot oven, 500°, for 20–30 minutes. Baste frequently with butter and wine.

Duck is best when quite rarely done. Also, many people do not realize that the oily skin can adversely affect the flavor. In the event your family does not like rare meat, leave the bird in the oven for 45–60 minutes at 450 degrees, basting at intervals.
—*The Great Outdoors*

CHERRY BRANDY DUCK

1 wild duck, cleaned (whole or quartered)
1 tablespoon sugar
$^1/_2$ tablespoon finely cut up crystallized ginger
dash salt
$^1/_2$ tablespoon orange peel, finely shredded
$^1/_8$ cup orange juice
1 tablespoon cornstarch
1 16-ounce can pitted cherries, drained (reserve syrup)
$^1/_8$ cup cherry flavored brandy

Preheat oven to 350°. Wash and dry duck. Brown in a small amount of fat in skillet. Place pieces skin side up in baking dish. In a small saucepan, combine sugar, ginger, salt, orange peel, orange juice and $^1/_3$ cup of the reserved cherry syrup. Heat to boiling and pour over the duck. Bake, basting occasionally with sauce, 45–60 minutes. (Duck is done when juices are no longer pink when meat is pricked with a fork.) Place duck on a warmed platter.

In a small saucepan combine remaining cherry syrup with cornstarch. Cook, stirring constantly, until mixture thickens and clarifies. Boil, stirring constantly, 1 minute. Add cherries and brandy to sauce. Heat through and serve over duck. Serves 3–4.
—National Rifle Association *Centennial Cookbook*

DUCK SOUP

1 large or 2 small ducks, cut into small pieces
8 cups water
2 stalks celery with leaves, chopped
1 large carrot, shredded
1 large onion, diced
1 teaspoon salt
6 chicken bouillon cubes
thin noodles, rice or barley

Place all ingredients, except noodles, rice or barley, in a large kettle. Simmer gently 2–3 hours. If too thick, add 1 cup water. Add 2–3 ounces thin noodles. Rice or barley is also excellent for thickening the soup. Cook very slowly ¹/₂ hour longer. Like most soups, this one is improved by reheating.—*U.S. Conservation News*

SAVORY PHEASANT

    2 pheasants, plucked and cleaned
    flour, seasoned with salt, pepper, and paprika
    butter
    2 onions, finely chopped
    ¹/₂ cup sweet vermouth
    1 teaspoon tomato paste
    ¹/₈ teaspoon cinnamon
    1 teaspoon salt
    dash freshly ground pepper
    soft butter
    buttered toast triangles

Cut pheasants into serving pieces. Dust with the seasoned flour and brown in butter. Transfer pheasant pieces to roasting pan.

To remaining butter in skillet, add onion and sauté until transparent. Add vermouth, tomato paste, cinnamon, salt, and pepper. Cook for 2 minutes and then pour around the pheasant pieces.

Spread soft butter on pieces of bird and roast for 1 hour at 350°, or until meat is tender. Arrange triangles of buttered toast on hot platter and pour a spoonful of sauce from the roaster on each piece. Place pheasant pieces on top and garnish with watercress.
—Gene Grey, Manhattan, KS (from Nikki Konitz, Lewistown, MT)

STUFFED ROAST PHEASANT

1 pheasant	juice of $^1/_2$ lemon
2 ounces butter	$^1/_2$ pound sausage meat
2 strips bacon	1 apple
1 wineglass of sherry	1 egg
1 tablespoon red currant	dried parsley
jelly	salt and pepper

Mix the sausage meat, apple, egg, parsley, salt, and pepper, and stuff the bird. Wrap bacon around it, dot with butter, and roast in a 350° oven for 45 minutes.

Drain off surplus fat and pour the sherry mixed with the jelly and lemon juice over the bird. Cook another 15 minutes, basting a few times with the sauce.—*The Great Outdoors*

PHEASANT TERIYAKI

2 pheasants, cut in serving pieces and soaked in salt water (4 tablespoons salt and enough water to cover pheasants. They should be soaked at least 4 hours before cooking.)

$^1/_4$ cup salad oil

$^1/_2$ cup sugar

2 teaspoons ground ginger or 2 tablespoons grated ginger root

3 garlic cloves, chopped

1 cup dry white wine

1 cup soy sauce

1 teaspoon dry mustard

Rinse pheasant and marinate in mixture of the other ingredients $^1/_2$ hour. Bake uncovered in the marinade in a shallow pan until fork tender, usually 300° for $2^1/_2$ hours. Baste occasionally with marinade to keep moist. Serve on a hot platter with fried rice. Serves 4–5.
—Nancy Krenz, *New Mexico Wildlife*

b   i   g   g   a   m   e

FIELD CARE OF GAME

In big game or small game hunting, a well-placed shot is one of the first steps in securing meat that tastes good. A poorly placed shot causes a great deal of suffering for you and for the animal, spoils a lot of good meat, and possibly results in loss of the animal carcass in the woods.

Three vital areas—the head, neck, and heart—are the most effective for a fast, clean kill. For an immediate kill, the heart shot is best.

To make sure the animal is dead, use a checking method such as eye reflex. If the animal is a big game species, stand behind it and touch the eye. Watch for a reaction to this stimulus; if none is observed, the animal is probably dead.

If it is a big game animal, tagging is the next step. Tie the tag to an ear and then tuck the rolled tag inside the ear. This prevents the tag from being pulled off or getting soaked with blood while the animal is being dressed out. After tagging, meat preparation should begin immediately. A knife, towel, meat saw, small piece of rope, small block and tackle, and plastic and cheesecloth bags are a help. A good knife is essential—I would recommend a knife with at least a three-inch blade because a blade this size seems the most versatile.

Many hunters believe that "sticking" or bleeding an animal is necessary. This practice dates back to our pagan ancestors who thought that blood was demanded by their exigent gods. Doesn't it make sense that if you are going to remove the viscera (entrails), the animal will bleed out? When you remove the heart and lungs, the large arteries of the body are cut.

There are even some cases where bleeding out may be detrimental. In warm weather, it increases the possibility of spoilage. The animal should be opened up and cooled as soon as possible, and bleeding out retards this procedure. If the head is to be mounted, many times the cape is damaged. If you have been unlucky and shot the animal in the abdomen, the blood from the thorax will help flush the abdomen clean.

The body of any mammal can be thought of as consisting of two compartments—the thorax and abdomen. These areas are separated by a thin muscle called the diaphragm. The thorax, which contains the heart and lungs, is surrounded by bone. The abdomen, the lower compartment, contains the liver, stomach, kidneys, large and small intestines, and other vital organs. It is surrounded by muscle instead of bone.

The next step is probably the most important. You are now going to remove the viscera or entrails. The head should be facing uphill, if possible. Turn the animal on its back with the hind legs split. An imaginary line is drawn from the sternum (breast bone) to the anus or vent. You are now ready to make the first cut.

Some people believe you should start at the rear of the animal and cut forward, while others believe you should start at the middle of the animal and cut toward the hind section. (I start from the back section and cut forward.) No matter which method is used, the general principles are the same. Never cut too deeply with the first cut—only through the skin.

Remember the abdomen is protected with muscles. After cutting through the skin, proceed carefully through the abdominal muscles. The entrails will probably protrude through the incision and appear light gray.

Be sure not to cut the entrails because they contain food materials in various states of digestion. These materials cause meat spoilage and impart a bad taste to the meat. An easy way to make a nice, neat cut without hitting the entrails is to place your second and third fingers in the incision with the palm facing up. Cut toward the breast bone.

The next step is to cut the diaphragm. As previously mentioned, this muscle wall is found within the body cavity and separates the thorax from the abdomen. After cutting the diaphragm, reach up as far into the thorax as you can and cut the esophagus (gullet) and trachea (windpipe). These are the large tubes found just in front of the vertebrae. To make this job a little easier, many hunters cut all the way up to the neck with a knife or small meat saw. If you use a knife, cut along the breast bone where the ribs have a cartilaginous attachment.

In many cases, you may not want to open the animal up entirely. For example, when you have to drag a large animal quite a distance. Dirt and debris will soil the meat in the thoracic cavity. However, opening the thoracic cavity aids in cooling the animal and should be practiced in warm weather.

After cutting the tubes, remove the entrails. The alimentary tract may be removed by pulling on those tubes and rotating them toward the hind section. The alimentary tract is like a large tube with two openings: the mouth and the anus. You have freed the attachment near the mouth; now you must disconnect it at the anus. There are several ways this may be accomplished. Take the tip of your knife blade and circle the anus. This frees the tract at the posterior end. Some hunters find that splitting the pelvis and removing the large intestine by this manner is easier.

Let me stress the importance of removing the reproductive and urinary tracts. Care should be taken in removing the bladder. If this thin-walled sac is broken, the meat will have a disagreeable taste. A small towel may be used to wipe the carcass out. If you are near a stream, wash out the inside of the carcass.

Liver and heart fanciers salvage them at this point. This is where the plastic bag will come in handy. The liver is found roughly between the stomach, diaphragm and back. The heart is in the thoracic cavity and is surrounded by a thin-walled sac. Cut through this sac and remove it. Remember to remove the blood from the four chambers of the heart and drain as much blood from the liver as possible. Place both of them in the bag and tie it shut with a small rope. The free end of the rope may be tied around a rib to keep the bag in the thoracic cavity.

The last step is to remove the scent glands—the metatarsals on the outside of the lower hind legs and the tarsals on the inside of the hind leg at the back. The function of these glands has not been ascertained. They secrete an oily substance which has a musky odor and may affect the taste of the meat. Many people remove these first, but the problem is that they forget to wipe their hands and knife and then touch the meat. Wherever the meat is touched, a musky odor and taste will remain.

The carcass should be placed so it will cool out as rapidly as possible. The best way is to hang it from a tree because air then circulates freely. Once again, if you planned the trip carefully, you remembered to place a small block and tackle in your pack. Hanging the animal will be relatively easy. Sometimes it may be necessary to move the animal a distance to find an adequate place. If it is impossible to hang it, place it over a bush or deadfall. Whatever you do, don't leave it on the ground. The natural body heat of the animal will spoil the meat if this heat is not dissipated.

Cheesecloth or game bags come in handy at this point. In warm weather they allow air to circulate around the meat, but prevent flies from damaging it. Game bags also help prevent dirt and soil damage, both in warm and cool weather.

The method just described may be used on any large or small mammal. The procedures and general anatomy are similar. Remember—in all warm-blooded animals, the body heat should be dissipated as rapidly as possible because it causes spoilage.
—Vince Yannone, Helena, MT

DEER STEAK À LA SHERMAN

(This is a recipe for those who think they don't like deer steak.)

> deer steaks, ¹/₂ inch thick, with all fat removed
> cracker crumbs
> beef bouillon powder

Bread the steaks with cracker crumbs and pound them with a meat mallet. Sprinkle beef bouillon powder on the steaks and pound some more. Fry quickly in hot, melted beef tallow, 2–3 minutes on a side. Serve hot.—Gene Sherman, Glasgow, MT

VENISON STEAK

Cut venison into serving pieces, flour and season well with salt and pepper. Brown on all sides in a heavy skillet. Add enough cream to almost cover the steaks. Cover the skillet and simmer for one hour. Make gravy from pan drippings. Serve with the following sauce:

> small jar grape jelly
> 2 tablespoons brandy
> dash cinnamon

Simmer the sauce in a double boiler and stir until smooth.
—Deanna Nelson, Glasgow, MT

VENISON ROUND STEAK

> salt, garlic powder, freshly ground black pepper
> bacon grease
> onion, chopped
> 1 cup milk
> 1 can cream of mushroom soup

Season the steak with the spices and brown in the bacon grease. Briefly sauté the onions in the same pan. Mix the milk and soup together and pour over the steak and onions. Simmer 25 minutes or until tender.—Mr. And Mrs. James Crepeau, Anaconda, MT

SWISS STEAK

round steak—use steak from any big game animal
flour
1 can chicken gumbo soup
³/₄ can water

Pound flour into the steak and brown in hot fat. Place steak in casserole. Add the chicken gumbo soup and water. Bake at 350° for 1¹/₂ hours.—Jim and Helen Ramsey, Missoula, MT

VENISON STEAK WITH CREAM

flour, seasoned with salt and pepper
venison steak
shortening
1 medium onion, sliced
¹/₂ cup cream, either sweet or sour

Roll venison in seasoned flour. Brown in about ¹/₄ inch of hot fat in a heavy skillet. Slice the onion onto the meat. Add the cream; cover and cook slowly until the cream has almost disappeared. —Joanne Mayala, Helena, MT

PEPPER STEAK

1¹/₂ pounds ³/₄- to 1-inch-thick steak—antelope, deer, or elk
¹/₄ cup salad oil
1 cup water
1 medium onion, cut in ¹/₄-inch slices
¹/₂ teaspoon garlic salt
¹/₄ teaspoon ginger
2 medium green peppers, cut into ³/₄-inch strips
1 tablespoon cornstarch
2–3 teaspoons sugar
2 tablespoons soy sauce
2 medium tomatoes
hot cooked rice

Trim meat and cut into 2 x $^{1}/_{4}$-inch strips . Heat oil in large skillet. Cook meat in oil, turning frequently, until brown.

Stir in water, onion, garlic salt, and ginger. Heat to boiling. Reduce heat; cover and simmer 12–15 minutes. Add green pepper strips during last 5 minutes of simmering.

Blend cornstarch, sugar, and soy sauce together; stir into meat mixture. Cook, stirring constantly until mixture thickens. Cut each tomato into eighths; place on meat mixture. Cover; cook over low heat until tomatoes are heated through, about 3 minutes. Serve over the rice.—Faye Ruffatto, Miles City, MT

BOLD GRILL STEAK

> 3 pounds 1$^{1}/_{2}$- to 2-inch-thick steak—antelope, deer, or elk
> 1 can beer
> $^{1}/_{2}$ cup chili sauce
> $^{1}/_{4}$ cup salad oil
> 2 tablespoons soy sauce
> 1 tablespoon prepared mustard
> $^{1}/_{2}$ teaspoon Tabasco sauce
> $^{1}/_{8}$ teaspoon liquid smoke
> $^{1}/_{2}$ cup chopped onion
> 2 cloves of garlic, crushed
> 1 teaspoon salt
> $^{1}/_{2}$ teaspoon pepper

Mix all ingredients except steak, salt, and pepper; simmer 30 minutes. Brush the meat with sauce.

Place steak on a grill 4 inches from medium coals. Cook 20 minutes on each side, basting frequently with the sauce. Season with salt and pepper after turning and after removing from the grill.
—Faye Ruffatto, Miles City, MT

SKILLET STEAK & VEGETABLES

6 steaks—antelope, deer,
   or elk
2 tablespoons shortening
1 teaspoon salt
1 can tomatoes
1 package spaghetti sauce
   mix with mushrooms

$1/3$ cup sherry
1 can whole onions, drained
1 can mushrooms,
   drained and sliced
   (reserve $1/4$ cup liquid)
1 can peas and carrots,
   drained

Pound meat until it is $1/4$-inch thick. Melt shortening in large skillet; brown meat. Season with salt. Stir in tomatoes, spaghetti sauce mix, and sherry; heat to boiling.

Reduce heat; cover and simmer 10 minutes, stirring occasionally. Add onions, mushrooms, reserved liquid, and peas and carrots. Cover; simmer 10 minutes.—Faye Ruffatto, Miles City, MT

STEAK PARMESAN

1 pound $1/2$-inch-thick steak
   —antelope, deer or elk
$1/2$ cup dry bread crumbs
$1/4$ cup Parmesan cheese,
   grated
$1/2$ teaspoon salt
$1/8$ teaspoon pepper

$1/8$ teaspoon paprika
1 egg
$1/3$ cup salad oil
3 tablespoons water
1 can tomato sauce
$1/2$ teaspoon oregano

Cut meat into 4 serving pieces. Pound until $1/4$ inch thick. Stir together bread crumbs, cheese, salt, pepper, and paprika. Beat egg slightly. Dip meat into egg, then into crumb mixture, coating both sides.

Heat oil in large skillet. Brown meat on both sides, about 6 minutes total time. Reduce heat. Add water; cover and simmer 30–40 minutes or until meat is tender.

Remove meat from skillet; keep warm. Pour tomato sauce into skillet; stir in oregano. Heat to boiling and pour over meat.
—Faye Ruffatto, Miles City, MT

STEAK DIANE

1 pound antelope steak
1 clove of garlic, crushed
$^1/_8$ teaspoon lemon juice
1 teaspoon Worcestershire sauce
$^1/_4$ cup butter or margarine
2 tablespoons parsley, minced
2 tablespoons butter or margarine
$^1/_2$ cup mushrooms, sliced
2 tablespoons onion, minced

Melt the $^1/_4$ cup butter; stir in the mushrooms, onion, and seasonings. Cook until mushrooms are tender. Stir in parsley; keep sauce warm. Melt the 2 tablespoons of butter in a skillet. Turning once, cook meat in butter over medium-high heat. Three to four minutes on each side will yield about medium doneness. Top with the mushroom sauce.—Faye Ruffatto, Miles City, MT

MARINATED MEATS AND VEGETABLES

1 quart canned meat—
  deer, elk or antelope
  may be used
1 jar mushrooms, drained
  and sliced
1 medium green pepper,
  sliced into thin rings
$^1/_3$ cup red wine vinegar
$^1/_4$ cup salad oil

1 teaspoon salt
$^1/_2$ teaspoon onion salt
$^1/_2$ teaspoon
  Worcestershire sauce
$^1/_4$ teaspoon pepper
$^1/_4$ teaspoon tarragon
2 cloves garlic, crushed
lettuce leaves
cherry tomatoes

Arrange meat in a baking dish. Place mushrooms on the meat and top with green pepper rings. Combine vinegar, oil and seasonings; pour over meat and vegetables. Cover; refrigerate at least 3 hours, spooning marinade over vegetables occasionally.

With a slotted spoon, remove vegetables to lettuce leaves on salad plates. Arrange meat beside vegetables and garnish with cherry tomatoes.—Faye Ruffatto, Miles City, MT

VENISON SOUP

2½ pounds venison—shank, flank, neck, or breast
2 quarts cold water
1 cup diced carrots
1½ cups diced potatoes
¾ cup diced celery
½ cup finely chopped onion
2 tablespoons finely chopped parsley
3 cups tomato juice
2 tablespoons salt
½ teaspoon savory
¼ teaspoon pepper
1 tablespoon sugar

Simmer meat in salted water for 2–2½ hours, skimming occasionally. Let broth stand overnight or until fat has congealed. Remove congealed fat and add vegetables, juice, and seasonings. Simmer slowly for about two hours.
—Ged Petit, *Tennessee Conservationist*

SHORTCUT STEW

1 quart canned meat—deer, elk or antelope may be used
1 large onion, chopped
1 clove garlic, minced
4 medium potatoes, pared and cut into eighths
1 can tomatoes
1 can tomato sauce
1 teaspoon salt
1 package frozen green peas
$^1/_2$ medium green pepper, chopped

Combine meat (with juice), onion, garlic, potatoes, tomatoes, tomato sauce, and salt; heat to boiling. Reduce heat. Simmer, uncovered, stirring occasionally, about 30 minutes or until vegetables are almost tender. Add peas and green pepper; heat to boiling, reduce heat, and cook 5 minutes longer. For thicker stew, shake $^1/_3$ cup water with 2 tablespoon flour and stir into stew.
—Faye Ruffatto, Miles City, MT

BURGUNDY STEW

$^1/_4$ cup shortening
1 quart canned meat—
    deer, elk or antelope
5 medium onions, sliced
$^1/_2$ pound mushrooms,
    sliced
1 teaspoon salt
$^1/_4$ teaspoon marjoram
$^1/_4$ teaspoon thyme
$^1/_8$ teaspoon pepper
$1^1/_2$ tablespoons flour
$1^1/_2$ cups Burgundy

Melt shortening; add onions and mushrooms and cook until onions are tender. Remove the vegetables.

Mix flour and the broth from the canned meat together, stirring constantly. After the mixture is boiling, stir in the wine. Add meat and spices. Cover and simmer 1 hour. Liquid should always just cover the meat. For the last 15 minutes, add the mushrooms and onions.—Faye Ruffatto, Miles City, MT

COMPANY'S COMIN' STEW

1–3 pounds of wild stew
  meat, cubed
1–2 pints sour cream
1–2 cans cream of
  mushroom soup
1–3 small cans mushrooms
¹/₂ cup flour

¹/₂ teaspoon salt
¹/₄ teaspoon pepper
¹/₄ teaspoon nutmeg
4 tablespoons shortening
1–2 pounds wide egg
  noodles
milk

Put flour, salt, pepper, and nutmeg into a paper bag and shake to mix. Place the cubed meat in the bag (double the amount of flour and spices for 2–3 pounds of meat) and shake to coat. Place meat in a heavy skillet and brown in the melted shortening.

Pour sour cream, cream of mushroom soup, and mushrooms over the meat and stir in enough milk to make a thin gravy. Cover the skillet and bake at 300° for 45 minutes to 1 hour. Check occasionally and add more milk to maintain the sauce at a gravy-like consistency; it will thicken as it cooks.

Cook noodles in salted water; drain and place in a large serving bowl. Pour meat and gravy mixture over them and stir to coat noodles. Serve immediately.—H. M. Burrell, Libby, MT

WILD STEW

2 pounds stew meat—use meat from any big game animal
1 tablespoon sugar
2 tablespoons quick tapioca
1 can tomato soup (Use a little water to rinse out can.)
desired vegetables—potatoes, carrots, celery, turnips,
  parsnips, cabbage, onions, etc.
salt and pepper

Mix all ingredients in Dutch oven. Bake in 250° oven for 5 hours. Don't remove the cover while cooking.
—Jim and Helen Ramsey, Missoula, MT

ROAST VENISON WITH BARBECUE SAUCE

2¹/₂–3 pound venison roast
1 cup catsup
¹/₂ cup chili sauce
¹/₄ cup vinegar
3 tablespoons Worcestershire sauce
2 tablespoons prepared mustard
2 tablespoons butter
1 tablespoon salt
1¹/₂ tablespoons lemon juice
¹/₄ teaspoon cinnamon
¹/₄ teaspoon allspice
¹/₂ cup chopped onion

Sear the roast in hot grease. Mix all other ingredients together and simmer 5–10 minutes. Cover the roast with the barbecue sauce and bake in moderate oven, 350°, about 2 hours.
—Joanne Mayala, Helena, MT

VENISON POT ROAST WITH VEGETABLES

3–4 pound venison roast
¹/₄ cup cubed salt pork or
    mild bacon
2 tablespoons butter
6 carrots
6 onions
6 potatoes
1 teaspoon parsley flakes
    or 1 tablespoon chopped
    fresh parsley
1 stalk celery, sliced
¹/₄ teaspoon thyme
1 cup tart fruit juice or
    cider
1 teaspoon salt
¹/₄ teaspoon pepper
1¹/₂ cups hot water
3 tablespoons butter or
    drippings

Lard the roast by inserting cubes of salt pork into small cuts in it. Heat butter in a Dutch oven or deep casserole and brown the meat on all sides. Add hot water, fruit juice, celery, parsley, thyme, salt and pepper. Cover and simmer gently for 3 hours on top of the

stove or in the oven at 350°, until meat is tender. If liquid gets too low, add water. About 1 hour before meal is to be served, add peeled potatoes, carrots and onions. Add a little additional salt for vegetables. When vegetables are tender, remove them and the meat to a warmed platter. Thicken liquid with 2–3 tablespoons flour added to the drippings (or additional butter).
—Charles Raymond, Georgia Game and Fish

BUD'S BARBECUED RIBS

3/4 cup chopped onion
1/2 cup salad oil
3/4 cup water
3/4 cup catsup
1/3 cup lemon juice
3 tablespoons sugar
3 tablespoons Worcestershire sauce
2 tablespoons prepared mustard
2 teaspoons salt
1/2 teaspoon pepper
approximately 8 pounds ribs—elk or other
1 can beer

Sauté onion in oil until golden, not brown. Add remaining ingredients, except ribs and beer, and simmer at least 15 minutes (30 minutes is better).

Place the ribs in a flat pan; pour 1 can of beer and about 1/3 of the sauce over them. Marinate overnight if possible, but a few hours will do. Cover with foil and bake in 350° oven about 45 minutes; do not drain off marinade. Drain after cooking and put on barbecue over coals, basting steadily with 1/2 of remaining sauce. (Use hickory chips for a smoky flavor.) Serve final 1/3 of sauce on table or pour over ribs on serving platter.—John E. "Bud" Phelps, director, Utah Division of Wildlife Resources, Salt Lake City

BARBECUED RIBS

3 pounds ribs—elk, deer, moose, antelope or bear
3 pounds pork ribs (use an equal amount of game ribs and pork ribs)

Cut into sections containing 2 ribs about 4 inches long. Mix:

1 teaspoon turmeric
2 teaspoons paprika
1 teaspoon dry mustard
2 tablespoons salt
1$\frac{1}{2}$ cups sugar

Barbecue Sauce

1 medium onion, finely chopped
$\frac{1}{2}$ cup finely chopped celery
$\frac{1}{2}$ cup finely chopped green pepper
3 tablespoons vinegar
5 tablespoons lemon juice
1 teaspoon Tabasco sauce
1 cup catsup
1 8-ounce can tomato sauce
4 tablespoons Worcestershire sauce
1 teaspoon dry mustard
1 tablespoon celery salt
1 teaspoon salt
1 teaspoon black pepper
1 cup water

Place spice mixture in a jar or sack and shake ribs in it until they are thoroughly coated. Place ribs in a large cake pan or roaster and bake uncovered at 250°. Turn often and sprinkle with spice mixture. When well browned, pour off the grease. Combine ingredients for barbecue sauce and mix well. Spoon half of the barbecue sauce over the ribs. Let brown until dark, turn, and spoon the other half over the ribs. Brown again and serve.
—Loren Netzloff, Eureka, MT

MARINATED ANTELOPE PATTIES

1¹/₂ pounds ground antelope meat
1¹/₂ teaspoon salt
¹/₄ teaspoons pepper
6 slices bacon
2 cloves of garlic, minced
¹/₄ cup salad oil
¹/₄ cup soy sauce
2 tablespoons catsup
1 tablespoon vinegar
¹/₄ teaspoon pepper

Mix garlic, salad oil, soy sauce, catsup, vinegar, and pepper together. Thoroughly mix together meat, salt, and ¹/₄ teaspoon pepper. Shape into 6 patties. Place patties in glass dish; pour garlic mixture over patties. Cover and refrigerate 30 minutes, turning occasionally.

Remove patties from marinade. Wrap a bacon slice around each patty; secure with wooden picks. Place patties on broiler rack and broil for 12–15 minutes. Or, cook over hot coals on a barbecue or hibachi for 10–12 minutes on each side.—Faye Ruffatto, Miles City, MT

GROUND ANTELOPE–POTATO SCALLOP

¹/₂ pound ground antelope meat
¹/₂ teaspoon salt
1 package scalloped potatoes
1 jar pimiento, drained and sliced
3 tablespoons chopped green pepper

Brown meat, mixed with salt; drain off fat. Follow the directions on packaged scalloped potatoes; add meat, pimiento, and green pepper.

Heat to boiling, stirring frequently. Reduce heat, cover and simmer about 30 minutes or until potatoes are tender. (One package of broccoli, partially thawed and broken apart, makes a colorful and flavorful addition.)—Faye Ruffatto, Miles City, MT

VENISON PAPRIKA

2 pounds venison (trimmings or other bits and pieces)
1/3 cup salad oil
1 clove garlic, finely minced
3–4 cups sliced onion
1/2 green pepper, sliced in strips
2 stalks celery, sliced
2 tablespoons paprika
2 teaspoons salt
2 cups water
3 tablespoons cornstarch
2 tablespoons water

In a heavy kettle heat oil and add garlic and onions. Cook slowly. When just tender, add seasonings, other vegetables, venison and water. Simmer, covered, until tender (approximately 2 hours). Mix cornstarch and water together and add to venison mixture. Cook a few minutes or until broth thickens. Serve with cooked buttered noodles.—Mrs. Carl Faller, Hamilton, MT

WORKING PERSON'S DELIGHT

1 quart canned meat—deer, elk, or antelope may be used
2 tablespoons flour
1/3 cup water
1 beef bouillon cube
1 cup water, boiling
1 teaspoon Kitchen Bouquet
Minute Rice

Prepare Minute Rice according to package directions; set aside.

Dissolve bouillon cube in boiling water. In a large pan, mix the flour and 1/3 cup of water together; add the bouillon mixture and canned meat. For color, stir in the Kitchen Bouquet. Simmer 5 minutes. Season to taste and serve over Minute Rice.
—Faye Ruffato, Miles City, MT

VENISON BURGERS

2 pounds ground venison
¹/₄ pound ground pork or mild sausage
1 medium onion, chopped
¹/₈ teaspoon black pepper
¹/₄ teaspoon marjoram
¹/₄ teaspoon monosodium glutamate (optional)
2 eggs, beaten
2 tablespoons melted fat
¹/₄ cup sweet cider

Blend venison, pork, and chopped onion together. Add seasonings and beaten eggs. Blend well. Form into small patties, about ³/₄ inch thick.

Brown hamburgers on both sides in fat. Cover, reduce heat to low and simmer for 10 minutes. Turn hamburgers. Add cider, cover and simmer 10 minutes more. Serve immediately.
—Charles Raymond, Georgia Game & Fish

VENISON MEAT LOAF

2 pounds ground venison
¹/₂ cup chili sauce
1¹/₂ teaspoons salt
2 tablespoons butter
¹/₂ teaspoon thyme
2 eggs

¹/₄ pound pork sausage
1 small can tomato juice
1 teaspoon pepper
1 cup bread crumbs
1 medium onion, chopped
2 stalks celery, chopped

Dump the whole deal into a mixing bowl and mix the devil out of it. Transfer to a buttered baking dish, cook up to 1¹/₄ hours at 400° and serve hot.—Ged Petit, *Tennessee Conservationist*

SPAGHETTI-VENISON CASSEROLE

8-ounce package spaghetti (Leftover spaghetti
   without sauce may be used instead.)
1 medium onion, chopped
1 tablespoon butter
dash of salt and pepper
1 pound ground venison
1 can cream of mushroom soup
1 small can mushrooms, drained
1 No. 2 can creamed corn (or ½ can, if desired)
grated cheese

Cook spaghetti according to package directions. (If using leftover, put aside in casserole dish.) Sauté onion in butter for a few minutes. Add meat, dash of salt and pepper, and cook until meat is thoroughly browned.

In casserole, place spaghetti, meat mixture, soup, mushrooms and corn. Mix together. Top with grated cheese. Bake in 200° oven for 1 hour or 375° oven for 30 minutes.
—Linda Morley, Helena, MT

EGG-VENISON CASSEROLE

6 hard-boiled eggs
1 pound ground venison, browned
1 can cut green beans
1 can cream of mushroom soup
⅓ cup milk
1 cup cracker crumbs
butter

Slice eggs. Place half of eggs and browned venison in bottom of casserole. Add half the green beans; cover with half the soup and milk. Add the remaining eggs, venison, and green beans; cover with remaining soup and milk. Top with cracker crumbs; dot with butter. Bake at 400° for 15 minutes.—Linda Morley, Helena, MT

ZIPPY CASSEROLE

    1 pound ground game meat
    4 ounces uncooked elbow macaroni
    1 can cream of mushroom or cream of celery soup
    ³/₄ cup milk
    ³/₄ cup catsup
    ¹/₂ cup grated cheddar cheese
    ¹/₃ cup chopped green pepper
    1 small onion, minced
    salt
    1 cup crushed potato chips

Brown the meat; drain off fat. Cook the macaroni; drain. In an ungreased 2-quart casserole, mix all ingredients together, except potato chips. Bake 45 minutes in 350° oven, covered. Uncover and sprinkle with potato chips. Bake 5 minutes longer.
—Faye Ruffatto, Miles City, MT

LEFTOVER PIE

    1 can whole kernel corn, drained (save liquid)
    leftover gravy from roast
    ¹/₄ teaspoon Tabasco sauce
    2 cups diced cooked venison, elk, or antelope roast
    4 medium potatoes, cooked and sliced
    1 medium onion, chopped
    dash of salt
    ¹/₄ teaspoon thyme
    1 double pie crust, ready for baking

Mix ¹/₂ cup corn liquid with the leftover gravy. Stir in Tabasco. Combine corn, chopped meat, potatoes, and onion in 2-quart casserole; sprinkle with salt and thyme. Pour in hot gravy mixture. Cover with pastry. Seal edges and cut slits in top of pastry to allow steam to escape. Bake at 425° for 25–30 minutes.
—Linda Morley, Helena, MT

STUFFED GREEN PEPPERS

3 large green peppers
1 pound ground game meat
1 cup dry bread crumbs or cracker crumbs
1/3 cup chopped onion
salt, pepper
1 8-ounce can tomato sauce

Cut a thin slice from the stem end of each pepper. Remove all seeds and membranes. Bring 1 cup water and 1/2 teaspoon salt to boiling; add the peppers and cook 5 minutes; drain.

Mix remaining ingredients together. Lightly stuff each pepper with 1/3 of the meat mixture. Stand peppers upright in ungreased baking dish. Cover; bake 45 minutes in 350° oven. Uncover and bake 15 minutes longer.—Faye Ruffato, Miles City, MT

MEAT AND MACARONI SALAD

1 pint canned meat—deer, elk, or antelope may be used
2 cups uncooked macaroni
1 cup diced celery
1/3 cup sliced olives—black or green
1/3 cup chopped onion
3/4 cup salad dressing
1 tablespoon vinegar
1/2 teaspoon prepared mustard
1 teaspoon sugar
1 can peas

Cook macaroni as directed. Drain and let cool.

Drain meat and cut up in small pieces. In a large bowl, mix meat, celery, olives, onions, and macaroni. Mix salad dressing with vinegar, sugar, mustard; add salt and pepper to taste. Blend salad dressing mixture with meat; add peas and toss lightly. Refrigerate until chilled. Serve on lettuce leaves or in tomatoes.
—Faye Ruffatto, Miles City, MT

DEER CHILI

¹/₂ pound pinto beans	1 pound ground lean pork
5 cups canned tomatoes	¹/₂ cup chili powder
1 pound green peppers, chopped	2 tablespoons salt
1¹/₂ tablespoons salad oil	1¹/₂ teaspoons pepper
2 garlic cloves, crushed	1¹/₂ teaspoons cumin seed
¹/₂ cup chopped parsley	1¹/₂ teaspoons monosodium glutamate
¹/₂ cup butter	1¹/₂ pounds onions, chopped
2¹/₂ pounds ground deer meat	

Wash beans and soak overnight in water 2 inches above the beans. Cook in the same water 2 inches above the beans until done; do not drain. Add tomatoes and simmer for 5 minutes. Sauté green peppers in salad oil for 5 minutes. Add onions and cook until tender, stirring often. Add garlic and parsley. Melt butter in large skillet and sauté meat for 15 minutes. Add meat to onion mixture and stir in chili powder; cook 10 minutes. Add this to beans and spices; simmer covered for 1 hour, cook uncovered 30 minutes.— Ed Dutch, Texas Parks and Wildlife

QUICK CHILI CON CARNE

1 pound ground game meat
1 small onion, chopped
1 cup chopped green pepper
1 28-ounce can tomatoes
1 can tomato juice
1 large can pork and beans
3 teaspoons chili powder (or more, according to taste)
salt, pepper

Brown meat, onions, green pepper. Add tomatoes, juice, beans, and spices. Simmer for 15 minutes.
—Faye Ruffatto, Miles City, MT

VENISON MEAT BALLS

3 slices soft bread
1/4 cup water
1 1/2 pounds ground venison
2 teaspoons salt
1/4 teaspoon pepper
2/3 cup finely chopped onion

1/4 cup butter
1 tablespoon flour
3/4–1 cup milk
salt and pepper for gravy

Soak bread in water for 5 minutes. Break into small bits, pressing out as much water as possible. Combine bread bits, ground venison, salt, pepper, and chopped onion. Blend lightly but thoroughly. Shape into small balls about 1 inch in diameter. Chill 15–20 minutes.

Brown on all sides in butter, turning frequently. Cover pan. Turn heat to low and cook for 15 minutes. Remove meat balls to separate pan and keep hot. Add flour, salt and pepper to pan drippings and stir well. Add milk, stirring constantly; simmer 3–4 minutes. Return meat balls to pan and simmer another 5 minutes.
—Charles Raymond, Georgia Game & Fish

ZESTY BURGER

1 1/2 pounds ground game
  meat
1 1/2 teaspoons salt
1 3-ounce package cream
  cheese, softened

1 tablespoon prepared
  mustard
1 tablespoon horseradish,
  drained
1/2 cup chopped onion

Mix meat, salt, and onion together; divide in half. Put one half evenly in ungreased 8-inch pie pan.

Mix cream cheese, mustard, and horseradish together. Spread over meat in pan.

Shape remaining mixture of meat into 8-inch circle. Place on top of cheese mixture and pinch the edges together to seal. Bake 55 minutes at 350°. Remove meat to a large serving plate.
—Faye Ruffatto, Miles City, MT

MEAL-ON-A-SKEWER

1 quart canned meat—
   deer, elk, or antelope
2 cups tomato juice
$^1/_2$ cup vinegar
$^1/_4$ cup prepared mustard
2 teaspoons sugar
2 teaspoons salt
$^1/_2$ teaspoon pepper

$^1/_2$ pound mushroom caps
1 large green pepper, cut
   in 1-inch squares
1 pint cherry tomatoes
$^1/_2$ pineapple, cut into
   1-inch pieces

Mix tomato juice, vinegar, and seasonings together. Place meat in a shallow glass dish and pour tomato juice mixture over it. Cover; refrigerate 2 hours. Remove meat from marinade; reserve marinade.

On 6 skewers, alternate meat, vegetables and pineapple. Place on grill, 4 inches from hot coals. Cook 12–15 minutes, turning and basting frequently with reserved marinade.
—Faye Ruffatto, Miles City, MT

SPAGHETTI WITH MEAT SAUCE

2 pounds ground game
   meat
1 medium onion, chopped
1 green pepper, finely
   chopped
2 cans tomato sauce
2 cans tomato paste
1 can ripe pitted olives,
   drained and sliced
3 cups water

1 tablespoon sugar
1 teaspoon oregano leaves
2 cloves of garlic, crushed
1 bay leaf, crumbled
2 envelopes spaghetti
   sauce mix with
   mushrooms
2 cans chicken broth
   (use in cooking
   spaghetti)

Mix together meat, onion, and pepper and cook until brown. Stir in remaining ingredients. Simmer $1^1/_2$ hours, stirring occasionally. Cook spaghetti in equal amounts of water and chicken broth until tender. Drain but do not wash. Serve sauce over spaghetti.
—Faye Ruffatto, Miles City, MT

LASAGNA

1 pound ground game meat
1/2 pound sausage
  (if desired)
1 can whole tomatoes
1 can tomato paste
2 cloves of garlic, minced
1 1/2 teaspoons oregano
  leaves
1 teaspoon sweet basil
2 cups cream style
  cottage cheese

1/2 cup Parmesan cheese,
  grated
3 packages mozzarella
  cheese, shredded
1 package lasagna
  noodles, cooked and
  drained
1/2 cup Parmesan cheese,
  grated

Brown meat; drain off fat. Add tomatoes, tomato paste, garlic, oregano, and sweet basil. Heat to boiling, stirring occasionally. Reduce heat and simmer, uncovered, 20 minutes or until mixture is the consistency of spaghetti sauce.

Stir together cottage cheese and 1/2 cup Parmesan cheese. Set aside 1 cup meat sauce and 1/2 cup mozzarella cheese. In ungreased 13 x 9 x 2-inch pan, alternate three layers of noodles, meat sauce, mozzarella, and the cottage cheese mixture. Pour reserved meat sauce over top; sprinkle with 1/2 cup Parmesan and the reserved mozzarella.

Bake uncovered at 350° for 45 minutes. Let stand 15 minutes before cutting.—Faye Ruffatto, Miles City, MT

QUICK NOODLE CHOP SUEY

1 pound ground game meat
1 small onion, chopped
3 1/4 cups hot water
1 can water chestnuts,
  drained and sliced

1 package Hamburger
  Helper beef noodle
  dinner
1 can mixed Chinese
  vegetables, drained

Brown meat with onion; drain. Stir in water, noodles, sauce mix, water chestnuts and vegetables. Heat to boiling, stirring constantly. Reduce heat; simmer uncovered 10–15 minutes, stirring frequently.—Faye Ruffatto, Miles City, MT

VENISON CHOP SUEY

1 pound venison steak,
  cut in thin strips
2 tablespoons salad oil
1¹/₂ cups sliced fresh
  mushrooms (or 4 ounces
  canned, drained)
1¹/₂ cups sliced celery,
  (sliced diagonally)
1 cup chopped green pepper,
  in ¹/₂-inch squares
¹/₂ cup sliced green onion,
  sliced diagonally in
  1-inch pieces
1¹/₃ cups meat stock or
  beef broth
3 tablespoons soy sauce
¹/₄ cup wine, preferably
  sherry
¹/₂ cup water
2 tablespoons cornstarch

Brown venison in oil. Add beef broth, soy sauce and sherry. Cover and cook over low heat 20 minutes or until meat is tender. Add vegetables; bring to a boil and cook 5 minutes or less. Blend cornstarch and water; stir into sauce. Cook, stirring, until clear and thickened. Serve over cooked rice.
—Rick and Sandi Wallestad, Lewistown, MT

CHINESE HASH

1 pound ground meat—
  use meat from any
  big game animal
¹/₂ cup uncooked rice
1 cup diced celery
2 medium onions, chopped
¹/₄ cup soy sauce
1 can cream of chicken soup
1 can cream of mushroom
  soup
¹/₄ teaspoon pepper
2 cups warm water
  (or more)
1 can Chinese noodles
1 can bean sprouts

Brown meat lightly. Add vegetables, rice, soy sauce, and pepper. Put soups and water into a large baking dish and add meat mixture. Blend. Cover and bake for 30 minutes at 350°. Remove cover and bake 1 hour. Add bean sprouts last half-hour. Cover with Chinese noodles and bake 15 minutes more.
—Jim and Helen Ramsey, Missoula, MT

TERIYAKI STEAK STRIPS

2 pounds venison, cut thinly
1 can beef consommé (undiluted)
⅓ cup soy sauce
1 teaspoon savor salt
¼ cup chopped green onions (including tops)
1 garlic clove
2 tablespoons lemon juice
2 tablespoons brown sugar

Cut the steak diagonally, across the grain. Mix the other ingredients to form a marinade. Pour the sauce over the meat strips and refrigerate overnight. Drain and broil 4 inches from the heat until tender. Do not overcook.
—Charles Raymond, Georgia Game & Fish

CHINESE PEPPER STEAK

1 pound thin steak—deer or elk
3 tablespoons cooking oil
1 clove garlic
1 teaspoon ground ginger
3 tomatoes, thinly sliced
2 green peppers, thinly sliced
3 tablespoons cornstarch
salt and pepper, to taste
1 teaspoon sugar
½ cup water
3 tablespoons soy sauce
1 tablespoon onion rings, cut from
    the green portion of scallions

Brown meat in oil. Add garlic and ginger. Cook over medium heat; add tomato and pepper. Cover and cook about 5 minutes. Add remaining ingredients, except green onion rings. Simmer 20 minutes. Garnish with the onion rings just before serving.
—Ellen Anthony, Stockett, MT

HAWAIIAN HAMBURGERS

1¹/₂ pounds ground meat
 —use meat from any
 big game animal
²/₃ cup canned milk
¹/₂ cup chopped onion
²/₃ cup cracker crumbs
1 teaspoon Alpine
 seasoning salt

Sauce
24-ounce can pineapple
 chunks, drained
 (retain liquid)
4 tablespoons cornstarch
¹/₂ cup vinegar
¹/₂ cup brown sugar
¹/₄ cup soy sauce

Mix all ingredients together to form patties. Brown in fat. Cover hamburgers with the sauce and simmer for 15 minutes or more.

Sauce: Mix ingredients with 1 cup reserved pineapple juice. Heat until thick and clear. Add pineapple chunks. Pour over meat mixture.—Jim and Helen Ramsey, Missoula, MT

VENISON HALPSES

1 large onion, coarsely
 chopped
butter
1¹/₂ pounds ground venison
2 strips bacon, cut
 into ¹/₄-inch pieces
2 eggs, beaten
1¹/₂ teaspoons salt
¹/₂ cup rice, cooked
¹/₂ teaspoon pepper
¹/₂ cup bread crumbs

cabbage leaves
2 tablespoons
 Worcestershire sauce
¹/₂ teaspoon salt
1 tablespoon minced
 celery leaves
1 No. 2 can tomatoes
3 teaspoons sugar
1 bay leaf, crushed
3 tablespoons butter

Sauté onion in butter. Place in large mixing bowl and combine with all other ingredients.

Scald cabbage leaves in boiling water to soften; fill with venison mixture and fasten with toothpicks. Mix other ingredients and simmer 5 minutes. Place cabbage rolls in a baking pan, cover with sauce and bake 2 hours at 300°.—Joanne Mayala, Helena, MT

VENISON SAUERBRATEN

2 pounds of venison chuck, round, or rump roast	3 tablespoons fat
1 cup vinegar	6 carrots
6 peppercorns	6 onions
5 whole cloves	1 cup sliced celery
3 bay leaves	1 tablespoon sugar
	10 gingersnaps, crushed

Trim all visible fat from venison. Place venison in glass dish with cover. Add peppercorns, cloves, and bay leaves to vinegar and pour over meat. Add enough water to cover meat; cover the dish and refrigerate for at least 5 days.

Remove meat from marinade. Reserve the liquid for gravy. Heat fat in heavy frying pan. Brown meat on both sides. Add vegetables and 2 cups of vinegar marinade. Simmer until meat and vegetables are tender, about 1 1/2 hours. Remove meat and vegetables from pan. Add sugar and gingersnaps to remaining liquid to make gravy.
—Charles Raymond, Georgia Game & Fish

BREADED CUTLETS (SCHNITZEL)

8 boned loin cutlets— venison or antelope	1/2 teaspoon salt
2 tablespoons flour	1/4 teaspoon pepper
3 tablespoons grated Parmesan cheese	1/4 teaspoon nutmeg
1 egg, beaten	1/2 cup milk
1 teaspoon minced parsley	6 tablespoons butter
	juice from 3/4 lemon

Wipe meat with a damp cloth; pound with the back of a knife or meat mallet until quite thin; dip in flour. Mix cheese, 2 tablespoons flour, egg, parsley, salt, pepper, nutmeg, and milk and beat until smooth. Dip floured cutlets into the batter. Cook over low heat in 4 tablespoons butter until golden brown and tender.

Remove cutlets to a heated platter and keep warm. Heat remaining butter (2 tablespoons) until darkened; add the lemon juice. Stir and pour over cutlets. Serves 4.—H. M. Burrell, Libby, MT

f   *i*   *s*   *h*

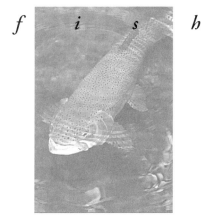

FIELD CARE OF FISH

The best tasting fish are those caught and promptly cooked on the streambank or lake shore—where the flavor is mingled with pine-scented mountain air and the pungent odor of campfire smoke. But this is a rare treat. Usually fish have to be transported home. Good field care is essential, since fish are among the most perishable foods.

Once caught, fish should either be killed promptly or kept healthy. Quality deteriorates if they die slowly. (Then too, it is more humane to kill them quickly.) Killing can be easily accomplished by thrusting a knife point between the eyes into the brain or by a sharp blow on the head. Once killed, the viscera and gills should be promptly removed.

Basic method for cleaning trout and salmon:

(1) slit belly from anal vent to gills,

(2) cut through lower junction of gills,

(3) pull out viscera and gills,

(4) run thumbnail along backbone to clean out kidney. Use a minimum of water in washing the fish since water softens the flesh and reduces the flavor.

To maintain top quality, fish should be placed in a refrigerator or packed in ice (chipped or shaved ice is better than block ice) in an ice chest immediately after cleaning. When the flesh absorbs water it softens and loses flavor; therefore, place fish in plastic bags before packing in ice. Also, the water should be regularly drained from the ice chest. In the absence of an ice chest or refrigerator, every effort should be made to keep the fish cool.

The usual procedure when stream fishing is to kill fish, field clean them and carry them in a creel. The old stand-by is a wicker creel with the fish buried in green grass, leaves, moss or something similar. A canvas creel is fine if kept wet so it cools by evaporation. On warm days, fish should not be kept in a creel for more than three to four hours. Plastic bags are fine containers for packing fish in ice chests and freezers but are generally unsatisfactory substitutes for a creel. A fish in a plastic bag carried in a pocket is soft and mushy in short order.

When lake fishing, fish may be kept alive in a cage in shallow water or on a stringer. But if the surface of the water is warm the time should be short, and deeply hooked fish should be killed promptly. A safety pin stringer is the best type to use, with the fish pinned through the thin membrane just behind the lower lip. It can still open and close its mouth, and if you decide to let it go, it will be practically unharmed. Do not string a fish through the mouth and out the gills because this will damage the gills and cause slow death. If you are using a boat, be sure to pull the fish out of the water when going at high speeds to keep them from drowning.

The cook can tell a fresh fish by the following: eyes bright, not sunken; skin shiny; flesh firm and elastic to the touch, bones not separating from flesh; fresh odor; and gills bright red, not gray.

As final preparation before cooking, some like to dress a fish by removing head, tail and fins. Or, it may be skinned, filleted, or steaked depending on the kind and size of fish and the cook's choice.

Fish with large scales must have the scales removed. Often skinning is desirable, particularly if the fish has a strong fishy or mossy taste, since the skin contains much of the odor and taste. Of course, the type of water a fish is taken from will influence its taste.
—George Holton, Helena, MT

SMALLMOUTH BUFFALO FISH STEAKS

1 pound smallmouth steaks, fresh or frozen
1 10³/₄-ounce can condensed tomato soup
2 tablespoons snipped parsley
¹/₄ teaspoon crushed dried basil leaves
6 thin lemon slices

Thaw frozen steaks. Sprinkle fish with salt and pepper. Place the steaks in well-greased shallow baking pan. Combine soup, parsley and basil. Pour over fish and top with lemon slices. Bake at 350° until fish flakes easily when tested with a fork, 20–25 minutes. Serves 3–4.—Leona Schrupp, Billings, MT

CRANBERRY CATCH

2 pounds, thick fish fillets
1 cup sliced celery
¹/₃ cup chopped onion
6 tablespoons margarine
  or cooking oil
4 cups soft bread cubes
¹/₂ cup chopped pecans
1¹/₄ teaspoons salt
1 teaspoon grated
  orange rind
¹/₄ cup orange juice

Cranberry-Orange Sauce
¹/₃ cup sugar
2 teaspoons cornstarch
¹/₂ cup orange juice
¹/₂ cup water
1 cup raw cranberries
2 teaspoons grated
  orange rind

Cut fillets into 6 portions. Cook celery and onions in 4 tablespoons margarine or cooking oil in a 10-inch frying pan until tender but not brown. Stir in bread cubes, pecans, ¹/₄ teaspoon salt, orange rind and orange juice. Turn stuffing into well-greased 12 x 8 x 2-inch baking dish. Arrange fish in a single layer on stuffing. Drizzle remaining 2 tablespoons melted margarine or cooking oil over fish. Sprinkle with 1 teaspoon salt. Bake in 350° oven 25–30 minutes, or until fish flakes easily when tested with fork.

To make Cranberry-Orange Sauce, combine sugar and cornstarch in a 2-quart saucepan and mix. Add orange juice and water; cook, stirring constantly, until mixture comes to a boil. Add cranberries and cook 5 minutes or until skins on cranberries pop. Stir occasionally. Fold in orange rind. Serve with fish. Makes 1 1/4 cups sauce. Serves 6.—*U. S. Conservation News*

TROUT WITH ALMONDS

    4 trout, each about 8 inches long
    flour, salt, and pepper
    1/4 cup butter or margarine
    1/4 cup slivered almonds
    3 tablespoons butter or margarine

Dredge trout in flour, salt, and pepper. Fry them in 1/4 cup butter or margarine until done. Remove to a platter. To the frying pan add 3 tablespoons butter or margarine and 1/4 cup slivered almonds. Cook the almonds until the butter is browned. Pour butter-almond mixture over the fish and serve immediately.
—Mrs. Liter Spence, Helena, MT

EASY OVEN FISH

    2 trout, 1-3 pounds each
    salt
    pepper
    paprika
    juice from 1/2 lemon or lime

After removing the heads from the trout, split the fish along the spine to the tail, but not through the skin. Lay the fish, skin side down, on a shallow, foil-covered baking dish and sprinkle with the spices; pour juice over the top. Place fish in a 425° oven. When all the juices around fish and in the pan are gone, the fish are done.

If a crustier top is desired, put under the broiler until brown. Remove the fish by sliding a fork between the skin and meat, leaving the skin on the foil.

This is an easy and delicious way to prepare fish that will please diners and dishwashers alike.—H. M. Burrell, Libby, MT

BARBECUED TROUT

4 7-inch trout
1 clove of garlic, minced
½ cup white wine
½ cup tomato juice
1 tablespoon soy sauce
½ cup butter, melted
½ teaspoon oregano
½ teaspoon salt
½ teaspoon pepper

Mix all ingredients together, except the fish. Place the trout, preferably freshly caught, on a grill about 4 inches above a bed of fine coals. Cook about 4 minutes without turning. Turn the fish and baste with the above sauce. Cook the fish no longer than 10 minutes.

Either spread the remaining sauce over the fish or serve it as a dip.—G. Earl Quinliven, *Outdoor California*

MONTANA TROUT BAKED IN WINE

3–4 good-sized trout, 8–10 inches long
6 tablespoons butter
¾ cup chopped onion
½ cup chopped parsley
1 cup dry white wine

Clean trout, leaving head and tail on. Sauté the onion and parsley in the butter. Spread ⅓ of the mixture on the bottom of a baking dish. Fill the cavity of the fish with ⅓ of the mixture and place the rest on top.

Pour the dry white wine over the top and cover. Bake at 350° until done (25–30 minutes). Uncover and sprinkle with bread crumbs. —Virginia Burns, Polson, MT

TASTY TROUT TREAT

cleaned trout

onions, carrots, and
   potatoes, chopped

parsley sprigs

celery, chopped

salt and pepper to taste

1 tablespoon butter per
   serving

1 tablespoon white wine
   per serving

Place cleaned fish on aluminum foil; add the vegetables. Sprinkle with salt and pepper; add the butter and wine. Wrap tightly in individual packages. Cook in 350-degree oven until the vegetables are done.

This package can also be cooked in campfire coals.
—Wendy Young, *Wyoming Wildlife*

PARADE-DRESSED WHITEFISH

2 pounds whitefish fillets or other fish fillets,
   fresh or frozen

1 teaspoon salt

dash pepper

2 tablespoons melted fat or oil

Thaw frozen fillets. Sprinkle them with salt and pepper. Place half of fillets, skin side down, in a well-greased 12 x 8 x 2-inch baking dish.

1 cup chopped onion

$^1/_4$ cup melted fat or oil

2 cups toasted or
   dry bread cubes

1 cup grated cheddar cheese

2 tablespoons chopped
   parsley

2 teaspoons powdered
   mustard

$^1/_2$ teaspoon salt

dash pepper

Cook onion in fat until tender. Add to remaining ingredients and mix thoroughly. Place the stuffing on fillets in dish and cover with remaining fillets. Brush fish with fat and sprinkle with paprika. Bake in a 350° oven 30–35 minutes or until fish flakes easily when tested with a fork. Serves 6.—*Water, Woods & Wildlife*

f i s h

PADDLEFISH WITH ONION RICE

3/4 cup onion soup
3/4 cup instant rice
12 ounces paddlefish, cut in 1-inch cubes
1 cup mushroom soup
1 cup water
1/2 cup mixed red and green sweet peppers and celery

Bring the onion soup to boil. Add the instant rice and stir. Cover for 5 minutes. Keep hot.

Parboil the paddlefish for 2 minutes. Drain. (Save the broth for pet food.) Add the mushroom soup diluted with the water. Bring to boil and simmer for 2 minutes. Pour fish mixture over onion rice. Garnish with the mixed vegetables. Serves 2–3.
—Nancy Olson, Billings, MT

PADDLEFISH SUPREME WITH NOODLES

1 cup cooked noodles
12 ounces thawed paddlefish
1/2 cup catsup
1/2 cup water
1 cup frozen peas and carrots
dried parsley

Cook 1 cup noodles according to directions on package. Spread in baking dish and keep hot.

Cut thawed fish in 1-inch cubes and place in a kettle. Barely cover with cold water and bring to boil for 2 minutes. Drain off the milky broth. (Save for pet food.) Add the catsup diluted with the water. Bring to boil and cook 2 minutes.

Cook 1 cup frozen peas and carrots until tender. Drain and add to the noodles. Spread the paddlefish on top. Sprinkle with dried parsley. Serves 2–3.—Nancy Olson, Billings, MT

PADDLEFISH HORS D'OEUVRE

Two ounces smoked paddlefish; if too salty simmer for 3 minutes in water. (Drain and let cool if the simmering step is necessary.) Shred 2 ounces cheddar cheese. Bind both together with salad dressing. Put small dabs on crackers and short pieces of celery. Arrange on a party tray.—Nancy Olson, Billings, MT

BROILED STEELHEAD

    fish steaks, about ³/₄-inch thick
    2 tablespoons finely chopped onion
    2 tablespoons butter
    salt and pepper, to taste
    ¹/₄–¹/₂ teaspoon marjoram
    parsley

After chopping the onion, cream it with about 2 tablespoons butter. Add the salt, pepper, and marjoram. Spread part of this mixture on the steaks; broil at 375° on a greased broiler pan. When browned, turn the steaks, spread other side with the mixture, and broil until done. (It will take about 5 minutes per side, depending on thickness of the steak.) Garnish with parsley and serve.

This quick, easy recipe works well with salmon, too.
—*Idaho Wildlife Review*

BROILED LING

Skin the fish and cut into 2 pieces. Place in boiling water and continue boiling 7 minutes. Remove to a broiling pan, coat the fish with butter, season well with salt and pepper. Broil until golden on top, 2–3 minutes. Garnish with fresh parsley sprig.
—Kay Christenson, Dillon, MT

FRIED LING

Prepare the fish as for broiling. Blend the following mixture together, place it in a paper bag and shake fish in it:

$1/2$ cup corn meal
$1/2$ cup flour
1–2 teaspoons salt
$1/4$–$1/8$ teaspoon pepper

Fry the coated fish in hot oil. The oil in the skillet should be deep enough to cover about half of the fish. In a large 12-inch skillet, this is at least two cups oil.—Connie Miller, Grand Junction, CO

BARBECUED LING

4 ling
4 slices bacon
1 small onion, chopped
$1/2$ clove garlic
1 bay leaf
$1/4$ teaspoon sweet basil
1 teaspoon salt
dash cayenne pepper
1 teaspoon brown sugar
3 ounces tomato paste + $3/4$ cup water
    or 1 No. 2 can tomatoes

Prepare ling as you would for broiling.

Fry bacon. Add onion and garlic. Sauté, until lightly browned. Add remaining ingredients to bacon mixture and simmer, covered, for 10 minutes.

Place fish in greased shallow baking dish and pour sauce over fish. Bake 1 hour in 375° oven. Serve over steamed rice. Serves 4.
—Connie Miller, Grand Junction, CO

FRIED CATFISH

> 6 skinned, pan-dressed catfish, about 1 pound each
> 2 teaspoons salt
> 1/4 teaspoon pepper
> 2 eggs
> 2 tablespoons milk
> 2 cups cornmeal

Sprinkle both sides of fish with salt and pepper. Beat eggs lightly and blend with milk. Dip fish into egg mixture and roll in cornmeal.

Fish may be fried at a moderate heat in a fry pan that contains 1/8 inch cooking oil—or they may be deep fried. Brown well on both sides. Serves 6.—*Michigan Natural Resources*

POTATO-COATED CATFISH

> 4 pan-dressed catfish, fresh or frozen
> 1 egg, beaten
> 1 tablespoon water
> 1 cup instant mashed potato flakes
> 1 envelope onion salad dressing mix
> salad oil

Thaw frozen fish. Season it with salt and pepper. Combine beaten egg with water. Combine potato flakes and dressing mix. Dip fish into egg mixture, then roll in potato mixture; repeat. Brown fish in hot salad oil on one side for 4–5 minutes. Turn carefully; brown on second side until fish is brown and flakes easily when tested with a fork, 4–5 minutes. Drain.—Leona Schrupp, Billings, MT

f i s h

SESAME CATFISH

2 pounds catfish steaks,
  fresh or frozen
1 cup buttermilk
1 egg, beaten
1 cup flour
1 tablespoon salt
1 tablespoon paprika

$1/8$ teaspoon pepper
1 cup ground pecans
$1/4$ cup sesame seed
$1/2$ cup margarine, melted
$1/4$ cup pecan halves
lemon wedges
parsley sprigs

Thaw frozen fish. Combine egg with milk. Sift together flour, salt, paprika, and pepper. Add to ground pecans and sesame seed. Add ingredients to milk; blend well. Place margarine in shallow baking dish. Dip fish in batter and place in baking dish. Place pecan halves on top of fish.

Bake in 350° oven for 25–30 minutes or until fish is golden brown and flakes easily when tested with a fork. Garnish with lemon wedges and parsley sprigs. Serves 6.
—National Marine Fisheries Service

CREAMY ONION CATFISH

2 pounds catfish steaks,
  fresh or frozen
1 teaspoon salt
$1/4$ teaspoon pepper
1 8-ounce bottle green
  onion dressing
$1^{1}/_{2}$ cups corn flake crumbs

1 tablespoon chopped
  parsley
4 teaspoons grated
  Romano cheese
$1/2$ teaspoon paprika
$1/2$ teaspoon salt
lemon wedges

Thaw frozen fish. Cut into serving-size portions. Season fish with 1 teaspoon salt and pepper. Combine crumbs, parsley, cheese, paprika and $1/2$ teaspoon salt. Dip fish in dressing and roll in crumb mixture. Place fish in a well-greased, shallow baking dish.

Bake in an extremely hot oven, 500°, for 15–20 minutes or until fish flakes easily when tested with a fork. Garnish with lemon wedges. Serves 6.—National Marine Fisheries Service

CATFISH GUMBO

$1^{1}/_{2}$ pounds skinned catfish fillets, fresh or frozen
3 tablespoons melted margarine or cooking oil
1 cup sliced celery
1 clove garlic, minced
$^{1}/_{2}$ cup chopped green pepper
1 quart boiling water
2 chicken bouillon cubes
1 16-ounce can tomatoes
2 10-ounce packages frozen cut okra
1 bay leaf
$^{1}/_{4}$ cup catsup
1 6-ounce can tomato paste
$1^{1}/_{2}$ teaspoons salt
$^{1}/_{4}$ teaspoon pepper
dash liquid hot-pepper sauce
cooked rice

Thaw frozen fillets. Cut into 1-inch pieces. Cook celery, garlic, and green pepper in melted margarine or oil until tender. Dissolve bouillon cubes in water. Add bouillon, okra, bay leaf, tomatoes, catsup, tomato paste, salt, pepper, and liquid hot-pepper sauce. Cover and simmer for 30 minutes. Add fish. Cover and simmer for 15 minutes longer or until fish flakes easily when tested with a fork. Remove bay leaf. Place a small serving of rice in bottom of bowl. Fill with gumbo. Makes approximately 8–10 servings.
—National Marine Fisheries Service

CATFISH CREOLE

1 pound skinned catfish
  fillets, fresh or frozen
1/3 cup margarine or
  cooking oil
1/3 cup flour
1/2 cup water
1 cup sliced celery
1/2 cup sliced green onions
  and tops
1/2 cup chopped green
  pepper
2 cloves garlic, finely
  minced
1 16-ounce can tomatoes,
  cut into small pieces

1 8-ounce can tomato
  sauce
1 1/2 teaspoons salt
2 bay leaves
1/2 teaspoon thyme leaves
1/4 teaspoon pepper
1 tablespoon brown sugar
1 tablespoon lemon juice
1 teaspoon
  Worcestershire sauce
1/4 teaspoon liquid hot-
  pepper sauce
1/4 cup chopped parsley
cooked rice

Thaw frozen fillets. Cut into 1-inch pieces. Brown flour in margarine. Remove from heat and cool slightly. Add water gradually and stir until blended. Add remaining ingredients except catfish and rice. Cover and simmer for 20 minutes or until vegetables are tender. Remove bay leaves. Add catfish and simmer for 10 minutes longer or until fish flakes easily when tested with a fork. Serve over rice. Serves 6.—National Marine Fisheries Service

CATFISH-POTATO SCALLOP

6 skinned, pan-dressed
  catfish, fresh or frozen
2 teaspoons salt
1/2 teaspoon pepper
4 cups thinly sliced
  cooked potatoes
1 10 1/2-ounce can cream
  of celery soup
1 cup dairy sour cream

1 tablespoon chopped
  chives
2 tablespoons chopped
  parsley
3 tablespoons chopped
  pimiento
1/4 cup water
6 slices bacon
pimiento strips

Thaw frozen fish. Clean, wash, and dry fish. Season them inside and out with 1 1/2 teaspoons salt and 1/4 teaspoon pepper. Combine soup, sour cream, chives, parsley, chopped pimiento, water, and remaining 1/2 teaspoon salt and 1/4 teaspoon pepper. Reserve 3/4 cup soup mixture for topping. Place alternate layers of potatoes and soup mixture in a well-greased, shallow baking dish. Place fish on top of potatoes. Spread reserved soup mixture over fish. Place one slice of bacon on top of each fish. Bake in a 400° oven for 35–40 minutes until bacon is crisp and fish flakes easily when tested with a fork. Garnish with pimiento strips. Serves 6.
—National Marine Fisheries Service

CATFISH PARMESAN

> 6 skinned, pan-dressed catfish, fresh or frozen
> 2 cups dry bread crumbs
> 3/4 cup grated Parmesan cheese
> 1/4 cup chopped parsley
> 1 teaspoon paprika
> 1/2 teaspoon leaf oregano
> 1/2 teaspoon pepper
> 2 teaspoons salt
> 1/4 leaf basil
> 3/4 cup melted margarine or cooking oil
> lemon wedges

Thaw frozen fish. Clean, wash, and dry fish. Combine bread crumbs, Parmesan cheese, parsley, paprika, oregano, basil, salt, and pepper. Dip catfish in melted margarine and roll in crumb mixture. Arrange fish in a well-greased, shallow baking dish. Bake in a 375° oven for 20–25 minutes or until fish flakes easily when tested with a fork. Garnish with lemon wedges. Serves 6.
—National Marine Fisheries Service

f i s h

CATFISH REMOULADE

3 cups cooked, flaked
  catfish
²/₃ cup olive oil or salad oil
¹/₄ cup prepared mustard
3 tablespoons vinegar
1 teaspoon salt
¹/₄ teaspoon liquid hot-
  pepper sauce
2 tablespoons paprika
¹/₂ cup minced onion

¹/₂ cup minced celery
2 tablespoons minced
  green pepper
1 teaspoon dehydrated
  parsley
1 hard cooked egg,
  finely minced
lettuce
lemon wedges

Combine oil, mustard, vinegar, salt, liquid hot-pepper sauce, and paprika. Beat until thick. Stir in onion, celery, green pepper, parsley, and hard cooked egg. Fold in catfish. Chill for 1 hour. Line cocktail glasses with lettuce. Portion catfish mixture on lettuce. Garnish with lemon wedges. Serves 6.—National Marine Fisheries Service

BAYOU CATFISH

6 catfish, approximately
  1 pound each
1 cup dry white wine
¹/₂ cup melted fat or oil
1 4-ounce can mushroom
  pieces and stems,
  drained
¹/₄ cup chopped green onions

2 tablespoons lemon juice
2 tablespoons chopped
  parsley
2 teaspoons salt
¹/₄ teaspoon crushed
  bay leaves
¹/₄ teaspoon pepper
¹/₄ teaspoon thyme

Clean, wash, and dry fish. Cut 6 squares of heavy duty aluminum foil, 18 inches each, and grease lightly. Place 1 fish on each square.

Combine remaining ingredients. Pour sauce over fish using approximately ¹/₃ cup for each. Fold foil over fish and seal edges of foil. Place foil packages on a barbeque grill, approximately 6 inches from moderately hot coals. Cook 20–25 minutes or until fish flakes easily when tested with a fork. To serve, cut top of each package and fold back. Serves 6.—*Michigan Natural Resources*

GEFILTE GOLDEYE

¹/₂ pound goldeye fillets, fresh or frozen
6 cups water
2 medium carrots, sliced
2 medium onions, chopped
1 tablespoon salt
¹/₈ teaspoon pepper
2 eggs
2 tablespoons ice water
2 tablespoons matzo meal or cracker meal
¹/₂ teaspoon salt
dash pepper

Thaw frozen fish. In large saucepan, combine the water, half the carrots, half the onions, salt, and pepper. Bring to boiling and simmer, covered, 30 minutes. Finely grind the fish and remaining vegetables. Place in large mixing bowl; add eggs, ice water, meal, salt, and pepper. Beat at high speed until fluffy. Shape into balls or fingers, using 3 tablespoons for each. Place in broth. Cover; simmer 20 minutes. Drain; serve hot or cold with Beer Sauce.

Beer Sauce
1 cup mayonnaise
¹/₄ cup catsup
¹/₄ cup beer
1 tablespoon prepared mustard
1 tablespoon lemon juice
¹/₂ teaspoon prepared horseradish

Combine all ingredients and chill.—Leona Schrupp, Billings, MT

POACHED CARP WITH HORSERADISH SAUCE

1 3-pound pan-dressed carp, fresh or frozen
1 medium onion, sliced
2 parsley sprigs
1 bay leaf
3 whole peppercorns
salt

Thaw frozen fish. Pour water into poacher or large skillet to depth of $1/2$ inch. Add onion, parsley, bay leaf, peppercorns, and salt (use $1/2$ teaspoon salt per cup of water). Bring to boiling. Place carp on greased rack and set into poacher. Cover and cook until fish flakes easily when tested with a fork, about 20–25 minutes. Drain, serve hot or cold with Horseradish Sauce.

Horseradish Sauce
1 cup dairy sour cream
3 tablespoons prepared horseradish, drained
$1/4$ teaspoon salt
dash paprika

Combine ingredients and chill thoroughly.
—Leona Schrupp, Billings, MT

ORANGE AND RICE STUFFED PERCH

4 fresh or frozen,
   pan-dressed perch,
   about ³/₄ pound each
¹/₂ cup chopped celery
2 tablespoons butter
   or margarine
¹/₂ cup uncooked long
   grain rice
³/₄ cup water
¹/₂ teaspoon grated
   orange peel

¹/₂ cup orange juice
1 teaspoon lemon juice
¹/₂ teaspoon salt
1 tablespoon snipped
   parsley

Sauce
2 tablespoons melted
   butter or margarine
2 tablespoons orange
   juice

Thaw frozen fish. In small saucepan, cook celery in the butter until tender. Stir in rice, water, orange peel, orange juice, lemon juice, and salt. Bring to boiling, cover and reduce heat. Simmer until rice is tender, 15–20 minutes. Stir in parsley.

Sprinkle the inside of the fish with salt. Stuff each with about ¹/₂ cup of the orange and rice mixture. Tie or skewer the fish closed and place in greased, shallow baking pan. Combine the butter with the orange juice and brush with fish. Bake uncovered at 350° or until fish flakes easily when tested with a fork, about 30–35 minutes. Continue to baste with butter and orange juice mixture during baking. Serves 4.—Leona Schrupp, Billings, MT

SMOKED FISH DIP

4 ounces smoked fish
1–2 tablespoons milk
1 3-ounce package cream cheese, softened
1 tablespoon snipped parsley
dash garlic powder

Remove skin and bones from smoked fish; chop finely. (You'll need about ¹/₃ cup chopped fish.) In a mixing bowl, gradually add milk to cheese and blend until smooth. Stir in fish, parsley, and garlic powder. Chill. Serve with crackers.—Leona Schrupp, Billings, MT

f i s h

SAUCY CHEESE-COATED PERCH

1 pound fresh or frozen perch fillets
$\frac{1}{4}$ cup all-purpose flour
1 egg, beaten
1 teaspoon salt
dash pepper
$\frac{1}{4}$ cup fine dry bread crumbs
$\frac{1}{4}$ cup grated Parmesan cheese
$\frac{1}{4}$ cup shortening

Thaw frozen fillets. Cut into 4 portions. Coat fish with flour. Dip into mixture of egg, salt, and pepper. Then dip into the bread crumbs and cheese, mixed together. In skillet fry fish slowly in shortening until browned on one side, 4–5 minutes. Turn and brown the other side until fish flakes easily when tested with a fork, about 4–5 minutes longer.

Sauce
1 8-ounce can tomato sauce
$\frac{1}{4}$ cup water
$\frac{1}{2}$ teaspoon sugar
$\frac{1}{2}$ teaspoon crushed dried basil leaves

Combine ingredients in a saucepan. Simmer 10 minutes and serve over cooked fish.—Leona Schrupp, Billings, MT

SESAME PERCH

1 pound fresh or frozen perch fillets
salt
$\frac{1}{2}$ cup crushed round sesame crackers
3 tablespoons butter or margarine, melted

Thaw frozen fish. Cut into 3 or 4 portions. Place in shallow baking pan and sprinkle with salt. Top with the crushed crackers and drizzle the melted butter over the top. Bake at 350° or until fish flakes easily when tested with a fork, about 20 minutes. Serves 3–4.
—Leona Schrupp, Billings, MT

j e r k y, e t c.

SUGAR CURE SMOKED JERKY

Choose meat of long grain so the pieces will be chewy. Bottom round, shoulder meat, and flank steak are good. Cut meat into strips approximately $^1/_4$ inch thick and $^1/_2$ inch wide. Cut with the grain in pieces as long as possible. Partially freezing the meat makes it easier to handle.

You can make your own curing salt (see recipe below) or use a prepared mix. I prefer Morton's Sugar Cure. To make jerky more peppery tasting, add 1 ounce white pepper to each 3 pounds curing salt. Instead of this you might want to try 1 ounce cayenne pepper per 3 pounds of salt to make it even hotter. Rub the salt on the meat and let it sit in a cool place (refrigerator) overnight. Don't let it freeze or sit in too warm a room.

Next, hang the meat in your smokehouse or lay it on racks— CAUTION: USE NONGALVANIZED RACKS TO AVOID FOOD POISONING. Here is how I smoke the jerky: Using alder or chokecherry wood in an iron fry pan over my heater (a double-burner electric hot plate), I bring the smokehouse to 150° and turn the heat off. The meat begins to dry and smoke condenses on it. When the smokehouse is cool, I give the meat a second smoking by bringing the temperature up to between 120 and 150 degrees. I retain this temperature and check the meat occasionally by cutting through a thick piece to see if it is dried throughout.

When the meat is dry (it takes from 3 to 5 hours), I let it stand in the smoker overnight and cool slowly so smoke will condense on it to add flavor. The jerky will have a deep red, rubbery look and will be dry, yet chewy, all through. It should be stored in a cool place out of the sun.

Note: although an old refrigerator makes a good smokehouse, one built of two-by-fours with $3^1/_2$-inch-thick walls works better. The heat is easier to hold and control in all types of weather.

Homemade Dry Curing Salt for 50 Pounds of Meat

Mix:

- 1 pound salt
- $2\frac{1}{2}$ pounds white sugar
- 6 ounces Prague powder or saltpeter

For hotter salt, add 1 ounce white pepper *or* 1 ounce cayenne pepper.—Don Malmberg, Helena, MT

SALTED SMOKE CURED JERKY

Any type of wild game can be jerked. Remove as much fat and connective tissue as possible from meat. Slice into strips approximately $\frac{1}{8}$ to $\frac{3}{16}$ inch thick, 1 inch wide and 6 inches long. If the meat is tender, slice with the grain. If it is tough, slice across the grain.

Combine:

- 2 pounds fine salt
- 7 ounces Lawry's seasoned salt
- 1 ounce garlic salt
- 1 ounce white pepper

Use the Lawry's salt container as a shaker to put jerky salt on the meat. Sprinkle jerky salt on one side of each piece. Put a little more salt on the meat than you normally do, but don't oversalt. Place the strips of meat in a crock, enameled pail, or plastic bucket with the salted side up and let stand for 12 to 24 hours. Do not rinse meat.

Place meat on trays in a smokehouse at 150° to 180°, using a non-resinous wood (chokecherry, apple or any fruit wood), for approximately 8 hours or until meat reaches desired smoked taste and dryness. Most people like their jerky with a little moisture—in this case, it should be removed from the smoker before entirely dry. This moister jerky must be stored in a freezer or it will mold. Jerky can be dried until it is hard. It can be stored without refrigeration—Jim Ford, Missoula, MT

OVEN-DRIED VENISON JERKY

3 pounds fresh venison $^1/_2$ teaspoon garlic salt
liquid smoke   1 teaspoon Alpine Touch
salt mixture: fresh coarsely ground
2–3 tablespoons salt   pepper
1 teaspoon brown sugar

Jerky can be made from scraps of meat left after butchering—use the pieces you would ordinarily grind up for hamburger. Any tough cuts also make good jerky—just partially freeze the meat and then slice it into thin strips or chunks across the grain.

Put salt mixture on one side of meat, brush the other side with a very little liquid smoke. Stack the meat in alternate layers in a flat pan, a salty side against a smoky side. Place another pan on top and weight it down to press out meat juice. Let stand overnight.

The next day drain off juice. Grind fresh pepper over meat. Place on oven rack at 250°, making sure you line the bottom of the oven with foil to catch all the drips. Leave meat for about 5 hours or until dry. (It may be dried up to 8 hours but it becomes drier and more brittle than I like it.) Store in closed containers in a cool place.—Susanna Fliger, Billings, MT

SUN-DRIED JERKY

Cut beef or game meat with the grain into strips 1 inch wide, $^1/_2$ inch thick, and 6 to 12 inches long. Place the strips in a salt brine consisting of 2 pounds of salt dissolved in 6 quarts of water and leave for 2 days. Remove meat from brine, wipe dry, and hang it in the sun to cure. This may be done by threading the meat onto a heavy twine or wire, and spreading the pieces apart so that the sun and air can reach them.

Cover loosely with cheesecloth to keep flies off. When the meat is dry, the pieces may be stored in a dry cool place that is protected from dust or insects.

Note: the meat should hang for approximately 3 days depending on weather conditions.—Utah State Division of Fish and Game, from "Venison: Field Care and Cooking"

SMOKING FISH

Many devices, from pioneer smokehouses to old refrigerators, have been employed by many smokery enthusiasts. Commercial, portable units provide a practical approach for those not wishing to jump into the craft on a wholesale basis. These units consist of a metal box approximately 18 inches square and 24 inches high. There is a removable wire rack inside which holds the meat to be smoked. In the base of the unit is a small, low-power, electric hotplate and a metal pan. The pan is filled with wood chips from fruit trees, such as apple or chokecherry, or hardwood sawdust or chips. This is set on the hotplate where it is slowly "fried" to produce the smoke necessary to cure the food.

Remove the scales from large-scaled fish. (Scaling is not necessary for trout.) Wash the fish well in cold water. Remove any bloody flesh, and be particularly sure to remove the dark kidney strip from along the backbone. Fish weighing $2^1/2$ to 3 pounds can be smoked whole, although larger ones should be reduced to more manageable chunks.

Pack the pieces in a glass, earthenware, or porcelain container— never in bare metal. Using the proportion of $3/4$ cup salt to a gallon of water, prepare enough brine to completely cover the fish. Depending on the size of the chunks, the fish should soak from 18 to 48 hours. Oversoaking is practically impossible, so if you're in doubt, use too much rather than too little time.

At the end of the brining period, any scum that has formed on the pieces should be washed away with cool water. Dry the chunks with a clean towel and arrange them on the smoking rack, taking care that no piece touches the one next to it. This will allow free circulation of the smoke. Let the smoking rack with its load of fish sit out in the open air about 2 hours while you prepare the smoker itself.

If you use sawdust, sprinkle a little water on it and stir until the moisture is evenly absorbed. Bone dry sawdust has a tendency to smolder too rapidly and may even flare up.

Load the rack into the smoker and turn on the heating element. In a few minutes the wood in the pan will begin to char. A large volume of smoke is neither necessary nor desirable. If the amount of smoke escaping from the contraption resembles a factory chimney, your smoke-producing material is being consumed at too rapid a rate, which can cause a bitter flavor in the final product. Instead, maintain a thin, constant volume of smoke, replenishing the wood or sawdust whenever necessary. Smoke for about 6 hours. For a really pronounced flavor, smoke about 12 hours.

During the smoking cycle, brush the fish very lightly, interior and exterior, with cooking oil on a pastry brush at half-hour or hourly intervals. Be sparing with the oil, because too much will seal the meat and prevent it from absorbing the smoke as it should.

At the end of smoking, the fish should have a warm brown color like worn saddle leather. Fish will keep in the refrigerator for 2 to 3 weeks or may be frozen and stored indefinitely.
—adapted from *NEBRASKAland*

PICKLED FISH

(Whitefish, yellow perch, bass, pike, or catfish may be used.)

Clean and wash fish well. May use fillets. If fish are under 12 inches, cut them crosswise into bite-sized pieces ($1/2$–1 inch long). If fish is more than 12 inches, cut lengthwise first and remove the backbone. Measure fish in a quart jar as you cut them up.

Put the cut fish into a crock or large glass jar. For every quart of fish add $5/8$ cup salt. Now cover the fish with full strength distilled vinegar and stir to dissolve salt. Leave the fish in this solution for 4–8 days, depending on size of fish. Four days is enough for small brook trout. Bones should be soft enough to chew easily.

Remove the fish from the solution and put into cold, clean water for about 8 hours. Then pour off water and rinse fish once or twice.

Pack the pieces loosely in jars or freezer boxes. Prepare the following pickling solution enough in advance so that it is cooled to room temperature before adding to fish.

> For every 2 quarts of fish prepare the following:
> 1 cup cider vinegar
> 1 cup sugar
> 1 cup water
> $1^{1}/_{2}$ tablespoon mixed pickling spices
> 6 orange slices, $1/4$ inch thick

Simmer the above sauce for 45 minutes in a covered pan. Bring to a slow boil and remove from heat. For each 2 quarts of fish, add 1 package of Knox gelatin softened in 1 cup of cold water, and stir well. Allow mixture to cool completely before adding to fish or the fish will get soft.

A slice of onion can be added to each jar of fish if desired. Strain spices out and cover fish completely.

Allow jars to stand at room temperature for several hours or overnight. Then put into refrigerator to chill. They will keep for months if kept in refrigerator. They may be placed in freezer boxes and stored in the freezer.—John S. Mest, Manhattan, MT

PICKLED WHITEFISH

40 whitefish
1 quart very hot water
2 cups salt
2 quarts white vinegar (not less than 5 percent acidity)
onions, thinly sliced

Clean and scale the fish; cut off all fins and the tail. Cut into $1^{1}/_{2}$-inch chunks. Make a brine of the water and salt; let cool. Add the vinegar and pour over the fish, completely covering them. Let sit 4–5 days. Pour off the brine and rinse with water. Pack the fish in glass jars, tightly, with a layer of fish alternating with a layer of thinly sliced onions.

1 quart white vinegar
2 cups sugar
2 tablespoons salt
1 tablespoon pickling spice
3 cloves of garlic

Mix the above ingredients; bring to a boil. Boil 5 minutes; let cool. Pour over fish, completely covering them. Let sit for at least 5 days; 2 weeks is better. The fish will keep from 6 months to a year in the refrigerator. Eat them as they are or add sour cream and serve over boiled potatoes. To store, use plastic wrap and a rubber band. A metal cover will rust.—Loren Netzloff, Eureka, MT

CAMPBELL'S PICKLED FISH

Scale and clean whitefish, remove heads and tails. Cover the bottom of a 1- or 2-gallon stone crock with *rock* salt. Add a layer of fish and cover the fish completely with rock salt; continue this process, making sure that each layer of fish is completely covered. Add no water. Let stand 10 days.

Remove the fish from the crock. Wash them thoroughly, inside and out, in fresh water and let them stand in cold water for 1 hour.

Depending on the amount of fish to be covered by the pickling liquid, blend:

2 parts white vinegar
1 part water
1 cup olive oil or other salad oil
1 cup white sugar

Bring the above mixture to a boil and pour over the chunked fish in the crock. (Wash the crock thoroughly after salt solution.)

When the mixture is temperate to the hand, add the following:

1 box (3–4 ounces) pickling spice
3 cloves of garlic, thinly sliced
3 medium onions, sliced in ¹/₄-inch slices
1 lemon, sliced

Stir lightly every other day. Let stand 8–10 days.
—Vern Campbell, Somers, MT

CANNED GAME

6 quarts of 1- to 2-inch cubes of meat—
    deer, elk, or antelope may be used
6 cubes fat pork
salt
1 tablespoon chopped onion, per quart (if desired)

Cold pack cubed meat in jars as tightly as possible. Add 1 cube of pork per jar, ¹/₂ teaspoon salt and 1 tablespoon onion. Seal jars; process in hot water bath for 3-4 hours. Meat will make its own juice. Makes 6 quarts.—Faye Ruffatto, Miles City, MT

j e r k y, e t c.

CORNED WILD GAME

1 –1½ pound pieces of deer, elk, or antelope
1½ pounds of fine salt
½ pound brown sugar
½ ounce saltpeter

Place the meat in a wooden barrel or crock. Cover it with cold water so the water is about 2 inches above the meat. Let stand for 48 hours.

Drain off the water and measure it; then discard it. Measure the same amount of fresh, cold water; to every gallon used add the above proportions of salt, sugar, and saltpeter. Boil the mixture for 15 minutes and skim it. Allow it to cool; when its completely cold, pour it over the meat. Place a heavy weight on the meat to keep it under the brine (after washing, a rock works fine). Store in a cool place. It should be done in about 10 days.—H. M. Burrell, Libby, MT

SALAMI

25 pounds ground deer meat mixed with pork fat (⅓ pork fat)
6 ounces Tenderquick
6 tablespoons brown sugar
½ cup salt

Mix well and let stand overnight.
Add:

6 tablespoons black pepper
3 teaspoons cardamon
3 teaspoons allspice
3 teaspoons garlic powder
2 teaspoons red pepper
handful of peppercorns

Mix well. Pack tightly in loaf pans and tin cans. Be sure to leave about 1 inch at the top so the grease doesn't run over in the oven while the salami is cooking. Bake 5 hours at 200°.
—Mr. and Mrs. James Crepeau, Anaconda, MT

MINCEMEAT

4 pounds ground wild
  meat
1 pound currants
2 pounds raisins
1¹/₂ tablespoons
  cinnamon
1 tablespoon allspice
¹/₂ tablespoon cloves
¹/₂ teaspoon nutmeg
salt, to taste

4 quarts apples, chopped
¹/₂ cup molasses
1 cup vinegar
2-3 pounds sugar
¹/₂ pound suet or other
  fat
1 small lemon, juice and
  rind (grated)
1 small orange, juice and
  rind (grated)

Combine all ingredients. Bring to a boil, stirring constantly. Simmer about 1 hour, or until mixture reaches the desired consistency. Place in clean jars and seal immediately; or, mixture may be frozen.
—Ellen Anthony, Stockett, MT

PEMMICAN

1 cup dried meat (jerky)
1 cup dried huckleberries
1 cup peanuts or pecans
2 teaspoons honey
4 tablespoons peanut butter
³/₄ teaspoon cayenne pepper

Pound the meat into powder or grind with a blender. Add the dried berries and nuts. Here the recipe can become really elaborate with dried raisins, apricots, and peaches added, too, but remember to add proportionate amounts of the other ingredients for each new fruit.

Heat honey and peanut butter to soften it, then blend with the mixture. Add the pepper and make sure it's worked thoroughly through the mixture. To go completely natural, pack the mixture in sausage casings available at meat counters or put the mixture in plastic bags or containers. Store in a cool, dry place and it will keep indefinitely.—*Montana Outdoors*

PRESERVING MUSHROOMS

The easiest way to preserve the morel is to dry it. Do not wash, but clean off any surface debris. Cut in half to inspect for insects and lay out on a clean window screen, either outdoors in the warm sun or indoors near direct heat. They will dry in a few hours if air circulation is good. When thoroughly dry, store in plastic bags or tightly closed jars. When ready to use, rinse well in warm water, then soak for about 30 minutes until plump. Use as you would fresh mushrooms.

Any mushrooms to be canned should be blanched in boiling water or steamed. Steaming reduces water content and more mushrooms can be packed into each jar. Pack jars and process under pressure about 30 minutes.

All mushrooms to be frozen should be treated the same way as mushrooms to be canned. The shaggy mane is most adaptable to freezing. They should be heated slowly so they make their own juices. Save the juices and pack them along with the mushrooms in freezing containers. Heat the mushrooms just long enough to shrink them a bit. They may be diced before freezing—when thawed they make a delicious cream soup, to which may be added potatoes, clams or other vegetables.—Fran Davis, Otis Orchards, WA

INDEX